CREATION

Remarkable Evidence of God's Design

Grant R. Jeffrey, Ph.D.

Frontier Research Publications, Inc.
P.O. Box 129, Station "U", Toronto, Ontario M8Z 5M4

Comments on Grant Jeffrey's
20 best-selling books

ARMAGEDDON	•	MESSIAH
APOCALYPSE	•	THE PRINCE OF DARKNESS
FINAL WARNING	•	THE SIGNATURE OF GOD
HEAVEN	•	JOURNEY INTO ETERNITY
FLEE THE DARKNESS	•	MYSTERIOUS BIBLE CODES
SPEAR OF TYRANNY	•	THE HANDWRITING OF GOD
TRIUMPHANT RETURN	•	SURVEILLANCE SOCIETY
WAR ON TERROR	•	BY DAWN'S EARLY LIGHT
PROPHECY STUDY BIBLE	•	UNVEILING MYSTERIES OF THE BIBLE
JESUS: THE GREAT DEBATE	•	CREATION

"Grant Jeffrey's book, *CREATION—Remarkable Evidence of God's Design*, is a required tool in the arsenal of the Christian activist. With his balanced approach of the Anthropic Principle and Intelligent Design, Dr. Jeffrey presents a clear creation apologetic."

Frank Sherwin, M.A., zoologist, Institute For Creation Research

"Grant Jeffrey has written an extraordinary new book, *The Signature of God*, that provides astonishing proof that the Bible was inspired by God. Grant is recognized as the leading researcher in Bible Prophecy today."

Hal Lindsey, Hal Lindsey Ministries

"The *Prophecy Study Bible* is a phenomenal publishing effort by one of America's premier prophecy experts. Comprehensive, understandable, and powerful. A great work!" *Dr. Ed Hindsen, Editor – Jesus Study Bible*

"*Prince of Darkness* was written by acclaimed Bible Prophecy teacher Grant R. Jeffrey. This unequaled masterpiece is the result of 30 years of intense research. It will stir you and inspire you as few books have. . . . It is extremely well written — extraordinarily researched and fascinatingly presented . . . this is the best book I have ever read on this subject." *Jack Van Impe, Jack Van Impe Ministries*

"Grant Jeffrey . . . is now a best-selling author throughout North America. . . . His breakthrough book was his first, *Armageddon—Appointment With Destiny*. . . . Bantam Books later picked it up, and it turned out to be their No. 1 religious best-seller in 1990."

Philips Parchaud, Book Review Editor, Toronto Star, August 1, 1992

"We are excited about Grant Jeffrey's new book. . . . Now the book with the latest information on prophetic fulfilment, the book of the nineties, is *Armageddon: Appointment With Destiny*. It will show that God is in control and, most importantly, it will also prove to be a powerful witnessing tool to those who need Christ." *David Mainse: Host, 100 Huntley Street*

Table of Contents

Acknowledgments

CREATION—Remarkable Evidence of God's Design is the result of thousands of hours of intensive research involving hundreds of books, countless hours of Internet research, and more than three decades of study of the Word of God. Although more than one hundred text books are quoted in the documentation in the Selected Bibliography and the End Notes, these books represent only a fraction of the authors and researchers who have influenced and challenged my thinking about the subject of Creation.

The Bible and the Christian and Jewish belief in God's supernatural Creation are under relentless attack in our generation in high schools, universities, seminaries, and the media. Yet everything we believe as Christians, our hope for salvation and heaven itself, depends upon the truthfulness and trustworthiness of the sacred Scriptures. I believe it is time to stand up and launch a vigorous defence of the inspiration and authority of the Word of God, especially as it concerns the evidence for God's creation of the universe. This research and documentation of the recent scientific discoveries that prove that our universe was intelligently designed and fine-tuned to allow humanity to flourish will prove that the Bible's account of Creation is scientifically credible.

My parents, Lyle and Florence Jeffrey, who have lived a godly life before their children, have inspired a profound love for Jesus Christ and an unshakable belief in the inspired Word of God. Over the years they have continually encouraged me on my own spiritual journey to share my research and studies that relate to the authority of the Word of God.

I dedicate the book, *CREATION*, to my lovely wife, Kaye, who is my inspiration, my faithful partner in our ministry, and the manager of our publishing company. As we travel the world together to complete the research and interviews for these book projects, she continually encourages my efforts to share this research.

I would like to express my special thanks to my editorial assistant, Adrienne Tigchelaar, and to my editor, Rick Blanchette, for their excellent editorial services. I am very grateful to several scientists who reviewed this book for scientific accuracy, including Frank Sherwin, M.A., a zoologist and research scientist at ICR, California. I am not a scientist as my doctorate is in Biblical Literature. However, as a researcher I have spent many years studying the compelling new scientific evidence that is rapidly destroying the athiestic, evolutionary philosophy that has dominated science and education in our generation. An intellectual and spiritual revolution has occurred in the last two decades as thousands of scientists discovered evidence in the fields of astronomy, physics, and genetics that disproves the evolutionary materialistic concept that blind chance and billions of years could account for the universe and life itself.

I trust that the information in *CREATION* will instill in you a profound sense of wonder at God's wondrous creation, and that it will restore your confidence in the total authority and accuracy of the Holy Scriptures. My hope is that the remarkable evidence presented in this book will bring about a new understanding of the glory and majesty of God as our Creator.

Grant R. Jeffrey, Ph.D.
Toronto, Ontario
October 2003

1

Introduction

One of the most profound statements found in the pages of the Bible appears in the very first verse where God declares that He alone is the Creator of both "the heaven and the Earth." The Scriptures declare in their opening words, "In the beginning God created the heaven and the Earth" (Genesis 1:1). This declaration is certainly the most controversial and important scientific statement made in the pages of Scripture. The implications of the existence of God as our Creator are overwhelming concerning the truth about the purpose and meaning of human existence in this Universe as well as the question of Who actually created the marvelously complex "heavens and Earth" that includes the awesomely complicated biological life that flourishes on Earth.

At some point in the life of every serious person we

each begin to ask the ultimate questions about the purpose and meaning of the Universe and human life itself. Why are we here? Why does the Universe exist? Is there a purpose to life in our Universe, or is our life simply a random accident? If the Universe and humanity were created purposely by a super-intelligent God, what is our relationship and responsibility to our Creator?

The ultimate question facing every intelligent person who confronts the conflicting theories of random chance evolution and God's purposeful Creation is this: How did our Universe, the Earth, and humanity itself come to exist at all? Did our Universe form, as evolutionary humanists and atheists claim, through random chance by naturalistic and mechanical forces alone that operate without any purpose or reason? Or, was our Universe and humanity the result of an intelligent design, a divine purpose, and the creative acts of a supernatural Creator as described by the Bible?

Our answers to these questions have significant spiritual implications for our lifestyles, our priorities, and for our future life throughout eternity. This book will explore the tremendous new discoveries of modern science during the last few decades that provide compelling evidence that a supernatural Creator created the Universe as well as the Earth and Who is vitally concerned with the lives of all humans who were created "in His image" as the biblical book of Genesis affirms.

This book will examine an unprecedented revolution in the viewpoint of the world's leading scientists that has occurred during the last five decades regarding the nature of the Universe and biological life as well as the question as to whether there is evidence of a supernatural Creator. Fifty years ago the vast majority of leading scientists believed that the discoveries of modern science had eliminated the need for a supernatural Creator. They believed that the Universe had existed forever and, therefore, there was no need to explain its beginning. If there was no Creation, then there was obviously no need for a Creator. Decades ago the majority of scientists believed that Charles Darwin's evolutionary theory of natural selection involving gradual change through accidental mutations over millions of years explained the extraordinary biological diversity of lifeforms as revealed in both the fossil record and in our world today. In other words, they believed there was no need for a supernatural Creator to explain the origin of our Universe because Darwin's theory of evolution as outlined in his *Origin of Species* (published in 1859) pointed to the materialistic, natural process through which all life, including humanity, came into existence.

Tragically, hundreds of millions of Christians, as well as millions of non-Christians, have accepted unconditionally that the theory of evolution as taught in the high schools and universities must be scientifically true. Logically, if evolution is true, then the Bible's account of Creation as recorded in the first two chapters of Genesis that totally contradicts evolution must be false and nothing more than a myth. These opposing accounts cannot coexist: Either Creation or the theory of evolution is correct. At some point in his or her life a Christian places their faith and trust for their salvation and eternity in the truthfulness of the teaching, life, death, and the supernatural resurrection of Jesus

Christ as recorded in the New Testament. Yet, if they have been taught that the Bible's statements in Genesis were actually false about God's Creation, how can they logically and confidently place their faith and trust for salvation and eternity in heaven upon the authority of Christ's promises of salvation as recorded in other passages in the same Bible? The problem is that millions of Christians in our generation who believe that evolution has been proven scientifically to be true have been tremendously weakened in their faith in Christ, whether or not they ever talk about that logical contradiction or even think about it clearly. The Bible warns us that "a double minded man is unstable in all his ways" (James 1:8). "Double-minded" means holding two totally contradictory thoughts in your mind at the same time.

I believe that one of the major reasons for the superficial nature of the faith of many Christians in North America and Europe is that their acceptance of the false theory of evolution has created a logical contradiction, a "double-mindedness" that inevitably weakens their faith in the authority of the Word of God and in Christ's promises. Ask yourself: Why is Christianity in North America like the Mississippi River—"a mile wide and an inch deep"? George Barna has spent years studying the beliefs, values, and activities of North American Christians in comparison to non-Christians. He examined 131 separate measures of attitudes, behaviors, values, and beliefs and concluded that there were no significant differences in the behaviors and beliefs of Christians and non-Christians.[1]

Tragically, this is the first generation of Christians in the history of the Church whose personal behavior does not significantly differ from the secular non-Christian world that surrounds it. I have concluded that the reason for this is that ours is the first generation of Christians who, as a result of their acceptance of evolution and the resulting logical rejection of the Genesis account of Creation, has a fundamentally compromised view of the authority and truthfulness of the Word of God. This "double-mindedness" or uncertainty regarding the Bible's truthfulness has significantly weakened the faith and commitment of our generation of Christians. That is why the information in this book that demonstrates that the Genesis account of Creation is scientifically true is so important to our generation of believers in Christ. The elimination of the "double-mindedness" regarding the truth of the Scriptures is vital for Christians in our generation to enable modern believers to acquire the life-changing faith possessed by millions of Christians in past generations who shared an unshakable faith in the authority of the Word of God from Genesis to Revelations.

The unquestioning acceptance and teaching of the theory of evolution by high schools, universities, and the media has produced a logical contradiction in the minds of a majority of Western Christians that seriously compromises their faith in the commands and promises of the Scriptures. Jesus Himself, speaking of Genesis, warned: "But if ye believe not his [Moses'] writings, how shall ye believe my words?" (John 5:47). Our generation of believers in the West is the first generation in the last two thousand years of the Christian Church to have faith in Christ and the Word of God and, yet, have deep reservations about the scientific accuracy of many biblical statements, especially the Genesis account regarding the Creation of the Universe and life. It is my sincere hope that the remarkable recent scientific discoveries made in astronomy, atomic physics, biology, DNA, and the world of nature as documented in these pages will restore your confidence that you can totally trust the scientific accuracy of the Bible's account of God's supernatural Creation of "the heaven and the Earth" and of humanity itself.

Implications of the Theory of Evolution

The main philosophical position that underlies much of the modern attack on the authority of the Bible as the inspired Word of God during the last fifty years is based on an almost universal acceptance of the theory of evolution. This widely accepted evolutionary theory itself is based on a materialistic assumption of atheism—that there is no need for a supernatural God and that everything in our Universe, including humanity, has accidentally evolved from dead, inanimate matter by random chance over billions of years.

This atheistic materialistic rejection of the existence of God and His role as the Intelligent Designer of Creation provides the intellectual climate within which the educational and scientific communities today espouse the theory of evolution. Moreover, the theory of evolution provides the only other logically possible alternative to Creation that can attempt to explain the amazing complexity of biological life on this planet. When people finally accept the overwhelming evidence that makes the theory of evolution impossible and scientifically untenable, they will be forced to confront the only other logical alternative: Creation. The Universe, life itself, and humanity are the purposeful result of a supernatural act of Creation by a superintelligent God that exists outside of time, space, and the Universe. The fundamental importance of this issue demands that we examine the mounting scientific evidence that the theory of evolution is about to collapse due to a total lack of fossil evidence together with the increasing evidence that evolution cannot account for the staggering complexity in the DNA genetic code that governs all biological life systems.

The real agenda of many of those scientists and educators who embrace evolution is to use it to destroy man's faith in the Word of God, divine creation, and the Christian faith. This fact is demonstrated by the very words of leading atheists and supporters of evolution. For example, Professor J. Dunphy wrote in his revealing article entitled "A Religion for a New Age" in *Humanist* magazine (an atheistic publication) about their plan to replace orthodox Christianity with their new atheistic religion called humanism: "I am convinced that the battle for humankind's future must be waged and won in the public school classroom by teachers who correctly perceive their role as the proselytizers of a new faith: a religion of humanity that recognizes and respects the spark of what theologians call divinity in every human being. These teachers must embody the same selfless dedication as the most rabid fundamentalist preachers, for they will be ministers of another sort, utilizing a classroom instead of a pulpit to convey humanist values in whatever subject they teach, regardless of the educational level—preschool day care or large state university. The classroom must and will become an arena of conflict between the old and the new—the rotting corpse of Christianity, together with all its adjacent evils and misery, and the new faith of humanism. . . . It will undoubtedly be a long, arduous, painful struggle replete with much sorrow and many tears, but humanism will emerge triumphant. It must if the family of humankind is to survive."[2]

Although many people are unaware of the conflict, a war is taking place today for the hearts and minds of millions of adults and children over whether or not we can rationally believe the Genesis account of Creation. The faith of millions of Christians in the authority and promises of the Bible is at stake. This topic is vital to all who wish to come to terms with the authority of the Bible because the Scriptures clearly teach that God created the heavens as well as the Earth, and He ultimately created man in His own image. This biblical doctrine of Creation that is taught from Genesis to Revelation is in fundamental contradiction to the atheistic theory of evolution that denies the existence of God and claims that man lives in an accidental Universe without purpose, plan, or design. If evolution is true, then the Bible and the words of Jesus Christ are false. It is as clear as that. However, if the Bible's account of Creation is true and Christ's acknowledgement of Adam is true, then evolution is false

The reason this subject is so important is the powerful contradiction that exists between the paradigm of Christianity and the worldview of evolution. They are so fundamentally opposite that there is no possibility that both theories can be true. This inherent conflict produces a dangerous double-mindedness in the minds of millions of Christians who have been educated from elementary school to university to accept the theory of evolution as if it was proven to be an absolute truth. If evolution is true, they therefore must logically conclude that the Genesis account of Creation must be a myth. However, at the point of their conversion to faith in Christ, Christians enter into a personal relationship with Jesus Christ as their Lord and Savior, based on their acceptance of the truth and authority of the teaching of the Gospel account about the nature of Jesus, His sacrifice on the Cross, His resurrection, and their hope for salvation, resurrection, and heaven. If they never receive credible scientific information that proves to them that the theory of evolution is flawed, they will continue to hold within their mind the unchallenged teachings about evolution taught to them through their schools, books, and television. On the one hand, they accept the unchallenged belief, based on their secular education, that evolution has been proven to be scientifically true and that logically, the Genesis account of God's special creation of the Universe and humanity must be false. On the other hand, their trust for their salvation, their peace of mind and their hope of heaven itself is based entirely on their belief that the Bible's account in the Gospels about Christ's death and resurrection is absolutely true in all of its statements regarding the nature of Jesus Christ, salvation, heaven, and hell.

Do you see the problem? If the theory of evolution is scientifically true, then the Bible must be fundamentally false in its teachings about Creation in Genesis. If evolution were true, then Jesus Christ would have to be mistaken when He spoke approvingly of the biblical account of the creation of the Universe and his statements about Adam as a real person. If evolution is true, then it would be illogical to trust your very soul on the belief that the Scriptures are totally wrong about Creation but are absolutely trustworthy regarding the rest of the Bible's doctrines, including salvation as well as heaven and hell. If the Bible is wrong about Creation, how can we know that it is telling the truth about anything else? This logical contradiction is seldom thought about consciously, but it is so profound that it cannot help but affect Christians' general confidence in the truth of the Scriptures and, thus, weaken their daily faith.

When we examine the lives, deaths, and statements of faith of Christians in past centuries, we find overwhelming evidence of an unshakable faith in Jesus and the absolute truthfulness of the Scripture. This confidence motivated millions of believers during the past centuries of persecution to face torture and bloody martyrdom for themselves and their families rather than deny their faith in Jesus Christ. Where did this resolute faith come from? What motivated these past believers to count their lives as insignificant in comparison to their utter confidence in the promises of the Lord Jesus Christ as taught in the beloved pages of Scripture? The evidence of history is overwhelming that Christians in past centuries were motivated by a profound love for the Scriptures and an abiding trust in the absolute authority and inspiration of the Word of God. This faith in the trustworthiness of the Bible motivated the reformer Martin Luther to stand before the German royal authorities in the 1500s, who held his life in their hands. Luther said to them, "Here I stand. I can do no other." It was the firm confidence of the Reformers in the absolute truth of the Holy Scriptures that motivated their rallying cry *"Sola Scriptura,"* an affirmation that their faith and doctrine were based "solely" on the divine revelation in the pages of the Bible.

One of the most influential writers who helped to establish the theory of evolution as the almost universally accepted truth of modern Western society was Aldous Huxley. Although Huxley often presented the scientific reasons for believing in an accidental godless Universe that developed over untold billions of years solely through random chance, the truth was that his underlying motivation for rejecting the Bible's claim of divine creation was something quite different. In an article entitled "Confession of a Professed Atheist," Aldous Huxley was quoted as follows:

> I had motives for not wanting the world to have meaning; consequently assumed that it had none, and was able without any difficulty to find satisfying reasons for this assumption. . . . For myself, as no doubt, for most of my contemporaries, the philosophy of meaninglessness was essentially an instrument of liberation. The liberation we desired was simultaneous liberation from a certain political and economic system, and liberation from a certain system of morality. We objected to the morality because it interfered with our sexual freedom.[3]

This remarkable admission reveals that Huxley and

his contemporaries' real reason for their commitment to the philosophy of evolution was to enable them to escape the moral implications of a Universe where God created humans who had a moral response to His decrees. The thought of their ultimate responsibility to their Creator was so hateful that Huxley and his followers did everything in their power to denigrate God, Creation, and the Bible that affirmed that we will all some day stand before our Creator on the day of judgment.

A Recent Revolution within the Scientific Community Regarding Belief in God

For more than a century, most scientists throughout the world have rejected belief in a supernatural Creator as an obsolete concept that is no longer relevant to explain the existence of the Universe and humanity. The vast majority of scientists believed that scientific discoveries had eliminated the need for a Creator. However, an intellectual revolution has occurred during the last forty years in the world of science. The remarkable scientific discoveries in the areas of astronomy, the nature of the atom, the intricate genetic information encoded within DNA that controls all biological organisms, and discoveries in biological science have combined to transform the world of science.

An article by professors E. J. Larson and L. Witham in the April 3, 1997, issue of the prestigious science journal *Nature* reported on a fascinating survey of the beliefs of leading American scientists. The survey asked a thousand top scientists very specific questions about their religious beliefs regarding a personal God. The survey revealed that 40 percent of the physicists, biologists, and mathematicians acknowledged that they now believe in God. Remarkably, the questions revealed that their belief was not in some vague metaphysical abstraction. Rather; they believe in a God as a Supreme Being who is involved in our earthly affairs and hears our prayers.[4]

This remarkable survey suggests that the extremely widespread atheism among scientists in past decades has given way to a growing number of top scientists who have encountered compelling evidence in their own field of research to convince them that there must be an intelligent Designer who created the Universe. Unfortunately, the discoveries and views of these scientists that have led to this remarkable shift toward belief in a supernatural God as Creator have not yet reached the high school and college classrooms or textbooks. The recent fascinating scientific discoveries in astronomy, the nature of the atom, and DNA that point to the intelligent design of the Universe and life could produce a similar revolution in the attitudes of millions of non-scientists as well. Unfortunately, these discoveries have not yet affected the awareness of the secular or Christian citizen who is unaware of the truly remarkable discoveries that have transformed science's understanding of our Universe and its origin.

One of the difficulties we encounter when we consider the question of Creation and the origin of life in our Universe is that we are confronted with the limitations of scientific inquiry. By definition, empirical science is the study of things in our Universe that can be measured and tested in a repeatable way by other scientists. If another independent scientist in another laboratory cannot reproduce an experiment, then this experiment fails the universal scientific standard of *repeatability*. The creation of our Universe is clearly a unique "one time only" event that cannot be repeated. Therefore, it is a real challenge for science to ever positively and authoritatively describe the process by which our Universe and life itself originally came into existence.

Astronomer and agnostic Dr. Robert Jastrow reluctantly acknowledged that compelling new scientific evidence provides overwhelming proof that our Universe was purposely created by a superintelligent Designer to allow humans to exist. Professor Jastrow wrote:

> For the scientist who has lived by his faith in the power of reason, the story ends like a bad dream. He has scaled the mountains of ignorance; he is about to conquer the highest peak; as he pulls himself over the final rock, he is greeted by a band of theologians who have been sitting there for centuries.[5]

Professor Frank Tipler, mathematician and physicist, struggled with the profound conflict that existed between the atheistic naturalistic assumptions that he had accepted all his life and the contradictory evidence revealed by numerous new discoveries that pointed toward the conclusion that the Universe was created by a supernatural intelligent Designer. Dr. Tipler wrote, in his book *The Physics of Immortality*,

> When I began my career as a cosmologist some twenty years ago, I was a convinced atheist. I never in my wildest dreams imagined that one

day I would be writing a book purporting to show that the central claims of Judeo-Christian theology are in fact true, that these claims are straightforward deductions of the laws of physics as we now understand them. I have been forced into these conclusions by the inexorable logic of my own special branch of physics.[6]

God as The Divine Watchmaker

An English theologian, William Paley, was the first person in recent centuries who articulated the "argument from design," in his 1817 book *Natural Theology*, to support the Scripture's claim that God purposely designed the Universe to be inhabited by humanity. In the early 1800s he declared, "There cannot be design without a designer."[7] Paley argued that a man who discovered a watch while walking in the forest would be forced by logic and common sense to acknowledge that the complexity, the materials, and the obvious purposeful and intricate design of the watch capable of measuring the precise passage of time led to the logical conclusion that there must be an intelligent purposeful watchmaker who originally designed and manufactured such an intricate and complicated device involving complex gears and springs. Since a complex timepiece such as a watch was one of the most complicated manufactured devices existing during his lifetime, Paley chose this example to demonstrate his argument. He wrote, "Contrivance must have had a contriver,—design, a designer."[8]

Rev. Paley stated that "if the parts had been differently shaped from what they are," the watch obviously could never have functioned at any level of effectiveness. He also noted that the argument from design is much more powerful when we contemplate the complexity of biology in comparison to a mechanical device such as a pocket watch. Paley wrote, "The contrivances of nature surpass the contrivances of art, in the complexity, subtlety, and curiosity of the mechanism.[9]

The first known example of the argument from design was actually written almost two thousand years ago. This was attributed to the famous ancient Jewish Rabbi Akiva (approximately A.D. 130) in his commentary, *Midrash Temurah*, chapter 3. For more than eighteen centuries, from the time of Christ until the 1859 publication of Charles Darwin's *Origin of Species*, the majority of people in the West accepted the biblical worldview that the Universe, our Earth, and life itself was the direct result of the purposeful creative act of God.

Professor Ed Harrison, a cosmologist, wrote in his book, *Masks of the Universe*, about the implications of the new discoveries about the nature of our Universe. Dr. Harrison wrote:

> Here is the cosmological proof of the existence of God—the design argument of Paley—updated and refurbished. The fine tuning of the Universe provides *prima facie* evidence of deistic design. Take your choice: blind chance that requires multitudes of Universes or design that requires only one. . . . Many scientists, when they admit their views, incline toward the teleological or design argument.[10]

The unavoidable problem atheistic evolutionists

face in arguing for the accidental random mutational development of the biological diversity in our world is the immense complexity of biological life. Any honest evaluator of Paley's watch must admit that such a complex engineered system as a manufactured watch cannot be subject to random accidental manipulation without running the almost certain risk of a change that would cause the watch to cease to function at all. The odds against any simple change producing a worthwhile alteration or improvement without a very intelligently engineered matching change in every other related system to keep the whole system in balance is absolutely nil! The introduction of any change whatsoever in the watch's complicated components of cogs and gears without an extremely well-engineered complementary change elsewhere to compensate for the new change will inevitably produce a disaster and the previously well-functioning watch will no longer keep accurate time.

If any change is introduced by random, accidental chance into any complicated system such as a watch, a computer, or an infinitely more complicated system such as a biological cell, the result will be total disaster and the complete breakdown of the original operating system. If you have had the experience, as I did when a teenager, of taking apart a radio or watch to observe its function, you have probably also found that the entire complex system ceased to function and could not be reassembled to function again. Imagine if you had removed or added a new cog or spring to the complex watch assembly; would you imagine that such a casually modified watch assembly would continue to function as an accurate timepiece? Or would it improve the normal function of the watch? Obviously the answer is no.

The astronomer George Greenstein, in his book *The Symbiotic Universe*, wrote about recent discoveries in astronomy and the nature of the atom that confirm the absolute impossibility that our Universe resulted from random chance and evolution. Dr. Greenstein wrote,

> As we survey all the evidence, the thought insistently arises that some supernatural agency—or, rather, Agency—must be involved. Is it possible that suddenly, without intending to, we have stumbled upon scientific proof of the existence of a Supreme Being? Was it God who stepped in and so providentially crafted the cosmos for our benefit?[11]

Tony Rothman, a physicist, wrote, in a 1987 article in *Discovery*, about the need for scientists to seriously consider the implications of the astonishing "fine-turning" of the most fundamental scientific forces of the Universe: gravity, electromagnetism, the strong and weak nuclear force—all the fundamental forces that define that nature of our Universe. He said:

> When confronted with the order and beauty of the Universe and the strange coincidences of nature, it's very tempting to take the leap of faith from science into religion. I am sure many physicists want to. I only wish they would admit it.[12]

This Book's Purpose

The Scriptures themselves describe the underlying spiritual reasons why men and women choose to reject the obvious evidence that surrounds us that points to the existence of a Creator. The apostle Paul wrote to the Christians in the church at Rome describing the spiritual rebellion that leads to the atheistic rejection of God. Paul states that the evidence for God's Creation is "manifest" and that the true reason for rejecting God's Creation is the underlying rejection of the spiritual implications of our acceptance of God as our Creator and ultimate judge.

> For the wrath of God is revealed from heaven against all ungodliness and unrighteousness of men, who hold the truth in unrighteousness; Because that which may be known of God is manifest in them; for God hath shewed it unto them. For the invisible things of him from the creation of the world are clearly seen, being understood by the things that are made, even his eternal power and Godhead; so that they are without excuse: Because that, when they knew God, they glorified him not as God, neither were thankful; but became vain in their imaginations, and their foolish heart was darkened. Professing themselves to be wise, they became fools. (Romans 1:18-22)

There are many people, both Christian and non-Christian, who believe that there is a fundamental contradiction between an educated rational worldview and the orthodox Judeo-Christian belief in the Bible's statements regarding God's Creation of "the Heavens and the Earth." However, as this book will demonstrate, the scientific statements found in the Word of God will now stand up to careful investigation in light of the remarkable scientific discoveries that have recently been made in the fields of astronomy, the birth of our Universe, the nature of the atom, and the unfolding of the genetic code in DNA. There is now, in fact, no inherent logical contradiction between the claims of Scripture and a rational scientific worldview. Two thousand years ago the leading intellectual culture of Greece carefully examined the claims of Christian Scripture and recognized that the Logos, "Jesus Christ," was truly the beginning and end of all truth and wisdom. After a lifetime of careful study of the profound teachings of Jesus Christ and a decade of review of recent scientific literature, I am convinced of the truthfulness of the Word of God regarding the Genesis account of Creation.

My challenge as a researcher and writer is to first gather the scientific discoveries of the last few decades in astronomy, atomic physics, genetics, the role of DNA, and the fascinating discoveries in biology. Then, my more difficult challenge is to explain this extraordinary new scientific knowledge discovered in the last few decades in terms that can be easily understood by the average person who has little scientific training. Long ago the writer William Thackeray wrote about the great challenges facing any author: "The two most engaging powers of an author are to make new things familiar, familiar things new." My challenge and my prayer is that I might take my discoveries in the exciting world of scientific research and to enable my readers to understand the profound implications of this research as it relates to the question of the meaning of the Universe, the reason why we exist on this Earth, and the truthfulness of the Genesis account of God's Creation of "the Heaven and the Earth."

The prophet Isaiah wrote these words thousands of years ago: "Produce your cause, saith the Lord; bring forth your strong reasons, saith the King of Jacob" (Isaiah 41:21). In the following chapters we will explore the fascinating discoveries in astronomy, the marvelous complexity of intelligent design that occurred during the first seconds following Creation, the remarkable nature of the atom, and the miracles of genetic information transmission through DNA. The scientific fraud of the theory of evolution will be exposed and repudiated in the words of leading evolutionists who now admit that Darwin's theory is impossible. In addition, we will explore the wonders of God's creation displayed in the glorious diversity of life in the sea, the air, and on land that display His supernatural intelligent handiwork. My hope is that the material in this book will strengthen your faith in the Creation of both the Universe and humanity as described in the Word of God, and will restore your sense of wonder in God's Creation as we contemplate the glories of His intelligent design as displayed in our world.

One of the first true philosophers of science of the modern era was the English philosopher, Sir Francis Bacon, who delved deeply into the mysteries of Creation in his search for the meaning revealed in the natural world. Bacon wrote:

No one should maintain that a man can search too far, or be too well studied in the book of God's Word or in the book of God's works; divinity or philosophy; but rather let men endevour an endless progress or proficience in both.[13]

In other words, Francis Bacon was committed to the belief that God revealed His nature and purpose through His inspired revelation in the Scriptures as well as in the glories of His Creation. Significantly, Francis Bacon wrote,

A little philosophy inclineth a man's mind to atheism, but depth in philosophy bringeth men's minds about to religion.

One of the greatest scientists of the last century was Professor Albert Einstein. A theoretical physicist, Dr. Einstein wrote,

The scientist is possessed by the sense of universal causation. . . . His religious feeling takes the form of a rapturous amazement at the harmony of natural law, which reveals an intelligence of such superiority that, compared with it, all the systematic thinking and acting of human beings is an utterly insignificant reflection.

My hope is that the material in this book will answer some of the questions in your mind about the beginning of this Universe and that it will reawaken your sense of wonder at the glories of God's creation. In addition, I believe the research discoveries outlined in the following chapters will provide compelling evidence that the theory of evolution has finally collapsed due to its lack of fossil evidence and its mathematical impossibility, as will be demonstrated in a later chapter. In addition, the evidence presented regarding the intelligent design of our Universe will demonstrate the truth of the anthropic principle—that our Universe reveals overwhelming evidence that it was purposely designed for humanity. Last, and most important, the material in this book provides powerful scientific evidence that the biblical account of Creation as recorded in the opening chapters of Genesis is scientifically true.

Three thousand years ago King David looked at the night sky over his Jerusalem palace and penned these inspired words:

> The heavens declare the glory of God; and the firmament sheweth his handywork. Day unto day uttereth speech, and night unto night sheweth knowledge. There is no speech nor language, where their voice is not heard. Their line is gone out through all the Earth, and their words to the end of the world. In them hath he set a tabernacle for the sun" (Psalm 19:1-4).

It is significant that the remarkable discoveries of modern science in astronomy, astrophysics, the nature of the atom, and the astonishing genetic code within the DNA double helix, have all been discovered within the last few decades, and have provided powerful proof of the intelligent design of the Universe, the Earth, and humanity itself.

Notes

1. George Barna, "The American Witness" *The Barna Report* Nashville: Word Ministry, Nov./Dec., 1997.
2. J. Dunphy, "A Religion for a New Age," *The Humanist*, Jan.–Feb. 1983, 23, 26 (emphases added), cited by Wendell R. Bird, *Origin of the Species—Revisited*, vol. 2, p. 257.
3. Report, June 1966. "Confession of a Professed Atheist," quoted in *Beyond a Reasonable Doubt*, Shmuel Waldman, Jerusalem: Feldheim Publishers, 2002.
4. E. J. Larson and L. Witham, "Scientists are still keeping the faith," *Nature* 386 (3 April 1997), 435-436.
5. Jastrow, R. 1978. *God and the Astronomers*. New York, W. W. Norton, p. 116.
6. Tipler, F. J. 1994. *The Physics of Immortality*. New York, Doubleday, preface.
7. William Paley, *Natural Theology*, London: Faulder & Son, 1817.
8. William Paley, *Natural Theology*, London: Faulder & Son, 1817.
9. William Paley, *Natural Theology*, London: Faulder & Son, 1817.
10. Harrison, E. 1985. *Masks of the Universe*. New York: Collier Books, Macmillan, pp. 252, 263.
11. George Greenstein, *The Symbiotic Universe*, (New York: William Morrow, 1988) p. 27.
12. Tony Rothman, "A 'What You See Is What You Beget' Theory", *Discover* (May 1987).

13. Francis Bacon, *The Advancement of Learning*, London: 1605.

2

The Wonders of God's Creation

But ask now the beasts, and they shall teach thee; and the fowls of the air, and they shall tell thee: Or speak to the Earth, and it shall teach thee: and the fishes of the sea shall declare unto thee. Who knoweth not in all these that the hand of the Lord hath wrought this? In whose hand is the soul of every living thing, and the breath of all mankind (Job 12:7-10).

One generation shall praise thy works to another, and shall declare thy mighty acts (Psalm 145:4).

In this chapter, we shall examine the wondrous

complexity of our created world, from the intricacies of the organs of the human body, to the complex and ingenious mechanisms found throughout the world of nature. Each of the examples of organs or species found here can only function in a certain precise way—to have a partially-developed organ or system would have been impossible and totally useless to the organism. To believe that any of these complex processes would develop by chance at slow stages through random evolutionary mutations takes a much greater leap of faith than it takes to believe that an all-powerful Creator made the world around us to function in such a precise and remarkable manner.

The Human Body: The Glory of God's Creation

Of all of the glorious examples of God's intelligent design found in our Universe, the creation of the human body is the most wonderful creation of all. Even those who profess to believe in the theory of evolution are confronted with the greatest challenge to their philosophy when they contemplate the incredible complexity of the thousands of separate but interconnected systems within the human body that are essential for its growth, energy, motion, waste disposal, reproduction, and the brain's awesome mental computational powers.

A book published by *Readers Digest* dealing with the complexity of the human body concluded,

> The most incredible creation in the Universe is you, with your fantastic senses and strengths, your ingenious defense systems, and mental

capabilities so great you can never use them to the fullest. Your body is a structural masterpiece more amazing than science fiction.[1]

King David wrote in the psalms about the wonder of God's creation of mankind: "For thou hast made him a little lower than the angels, and hast crowned him with glory and honour. Thou madest him to have dominion over the works of thy hands; thou hast put all things under his feet" (Psalm 8:5-6).

The brain

The human brain is the most complex structure that is known to exist on Earth. Dr. Isaac Asimov, the late biochemist and atheist, wrote about the complex nature of the human brain in the science journal *Smithsonian*: "In man is a three-pound brain which, as far as we know, is the most complex and orderly arrangement of matter in the Universe."[2]

The complexity and intricate order found in the human brain almost defies our comprehension. When we consider the remarkable new discoveries in the last few decades regarding the powerful computational and memory capabilities of the brain, we feel an overwhelming sense of wonder at the glories of God's creation. Professors Fred Hoyle and Chandra Wickramasinghe wrote in their book *Evolution from Space:*

> The human brain consists of about ten thousand million nerve cells. Each nerve cell puts out between ten thousand and one hundred thousand connecting fibers by which it makes contact with other nerve cells in the brain. Altogether the

total number of connections in the human brain approaches 10^{15} or a thousand million million. Numbers in the order of 10^{15} are of course completely beyond comprehension.[3]

The hundred billion neurons in our brain are intricately linked to each other in the most intricate and complex network in the known Universe. Every one of these billions of neurons is connected to other neurons in a staggering number of complicated interconnections. Every single neuron is directly connected with more than fifty thousand other neurons through the incredibly small fibers, called dendrites, allowing instantaneous transfers of messages across your brain. There are more than one quadrillion intricate electrical connections, or synapses, within the brain, making it the most phenomenally complex machinery scientists have discovered in the Universe. Incredibly, although this awesome network of billions of interconnected neurons is the most powerful computer known to science, it exists within the 100 billion neuron cells that comprise only 10 percent of the three pounds of cells that make up the human brain. The other 90 percent of our brain is composed of almost a trillion glial cells that were previously assumed to perform only a supporting function to the neurons. Recent research, however, suggests that the trillion glial cells may play a very important function in the staggering number of calculations performed by the brain every second.

In less than one second, your brain can calculate the trajectory of a football thrown at thirty miles an hour toward you by your friend without any prior warning whatsoever. Your brain instantly calculates your position and the ball's trajectory, and sends detailed electronic messages to the muscles in your arms and legs at more than three hundred miles a second to move you into position to catch the ball. Despite billions of dollars and fifty years of advanced research on the brain by computer scientists seeking to duplicate its functions, there is no computer on Earth that can equal this marvelous instantaneous computing that is required to allow you to catch a football! Any fair-minded observer will conclude that the awesomely designed human brain must have been designed and created by God exactly as revealed in the Bible.

The eye

Evolutionists believe that the complex systems found in living creatures were formed accidentally as a result of random-chance mutations. However, the Bible reported that King David acknowledged God's miraculous handiwork when he wrote: "You have formed my inward parts; You have covered me in my mother's womb. I will praise you, for I am fearfully and wonderfully made" (Psalm 139:13-14, NKJV). Three thousand years ago, the wisest man in the world, King Solomon, wrote, "The hearing ear, and the seeing eye, the Lord hath made even both of them" (Proverbs 20:12).

Consider the case of the human eye and ask yourself whether or not such a complex and intricate optical system could ever have developed through random-chance mutation alone. When a baby is conceived in its mother's womb, the genetic DNA code governing the eye programs the baby's body to begin growing optic nerves simultaneously from both the optic center of the brain and from the eye. A million microscopic optic nerves begin growing from the eye through the flesh toward the optical section of the baby's brain. Simultaneously, a million optic nerves, with a protective sheath similar to a fiber-optic cable, begin growing through the flesh towards the baby's eye. Each of these one-million optic nerves must find and match up to its precise mate to enable vision to function perfectly.

We are generally impressed when highway engineers are able to correctly align two thirty-foot-wide tunnels dug from opposite sides of a mountain to meet precisely in the center of the mountain. However, every day, hundreds of thousands of children are born with the ability to see, their bodies having precisely aligned one million separate optic nerves from each eye to meet their matching optic-nerve endings growing out from the baby's brain. Anyone who thinks this miracle of design happens by chance probably still believes in Santa Claus. It astonishes the mind of anyone who begins to contemplate the scientific research that has been conducted on the eye's amazing construction and activity. The degree of complexity displayed in the construction of the various parts of the eye makes the evolutionary theory that it "evolved over millions of years by tiny chance mutations" an absolute impossibility.

Charles Darwin himself admitted that the intricate engineering displayed in the human eye was so specialized and complex that he could not begin to imagine how the eye might have developed through the evolutionary processes of natural selection.

To suppose that the eye with all its inimitable contrivances for adjusting the focus to different distances, for admitting different amounts of light, and for the correction of spherical and chromatic aberration, could have been formed by natural selection, seems, I freely confess, absurd in the highest degree.[4]

In a 1861 private letter, Charles Darwin allegedly wrote to American biologist Asa Gray (only a few years after writing *The Origin of Species*) about his growing personal doubts that evolution could ever have produced anything as complex as the human eye. "The eye to this day, gives me a cold shudder" because it is an "organ of extreme perfection."[5]

Another evolutionary scientist, Dr. Ernst Mayer, admitted the difficulty in imagining how the complex human eye could possibly form through chance mutations. "It is a considerable strain on one's credulity to assume that finely balanced systems such as certain sense organs (the eye of vertebrates or the feathers of birds) could be improved by random mutations."[6] One of the greatest problems facing those who deny a Creator is to explain how natural selection or random mutation could evolve such a phenomenally complex organ as the human eye when none of the hundreds of thousands of imagined intermediate mutations could have any survival value whatever until the completed optical system was in place to allow vision to take place. The only rational conclusion is that God instantly created the fully developed human eye when He first created Adam and Eve. *(See picture section, figure 1.)*

Recent research reveals that the human eye is much more complex and sophisticated than any camera designed by man. Similar to our advanced cameras, the human eye displays advanced auto-focus features with a remarkable ability to adjust the diaphragm of the iris automatically and at a phenomenal speed. The lens of your eye modifies its shape through tiny muscles that allow the eye to correctly focus on an object that is moving toward you or away from you. This action is similar to a sophisticated, computer-controlled modern camera when it calculates distances and automatically adjusts the lens to bring the object into focus. The lens of your eye is constructed of microscopic and transparent living cells. These cells allow light photons to enter through the cornea, pass through the optical fluid, then to be analyzed by the phenomenal organ known as the retina.

To appreciate the complexity and sophistication of the design of the eye, we need to understand the function of the retina. The retina lines the back of the eye and acts as a type of film, receiving the actual image composed of light photons passing through the iris, cornea, and eye fluid. Your retina is thinner than paper, yet its tiny surface (only one inch square) contains 137 million light-sensitive cells. Approximately 95 percent of these cells are rods that can analyze black-and-white images, while the balance of approximately seven million cone cells analyze color images. Each of these millions of cells is separately connected to the optic nerve, which transmits the signal to your brain at approximately three hundred miles per hour. The millions of specialized cells in your eye can analyze more than one million messages a second, and then transmit the data to the brain.

The retina in your eye is the most light-sensitive object in the Universe. It is more sophisticated in its design than even the most powerful electron microscope or satellite spy camera. For example, the most advanced film available today can differentiate between a range of one thousand to one. However, recent experiments have confirmed that the retina of the human eye can easily differentiate and analyze a range of ten billion to one. Experiments have revealed that the retina can actually detect one single photon of light in a dark room, something far beyond the range of engineered optical instruments. Recently, scientists discovered that the specialized cells in the retina actually partially analyze the image in the eye before it is transmitted through the optic nerve to the brain. While the optical image initially received in the eye is upside-down, the complex cells in the retina corrects the image to right-side up within the eye before transmitting the image to the brain. These retina cells perform up to ten billion calculations per second in determining the nature of the image transmitted to the eye by light photons. No supercomputer on Earth is capable of matching these virtually instantaneous calculations.

Dr. John Stevens made the following comparison in an article in *Byte* computer magazine in April 1985:

> To simulate 10 milliseconds of the complete processing of even a single nerve cell from the retina would require the solution of about 500 simultaneous non-linear differential equations

one hundred times and would take at least several minutes of processing time on a Cray super computer. Keeping in mind that there are 10 million or more such cells interacting with each other in complex ways it would take a minimum of a hundred years of Cray time to simulate what takes place in your eye many times every second.[7]

In his article, Dr. Stevens wrote that if we were to attempt to duplicate the computing power of the human eye, we would have to build the world's most advanced computer with a single enormous silicon chip (usually the size of a dime) that would cover 10,000 cubic inches and contain billions of transistors and hundreds of miles of circuit traces. The retina is so small that it fills only 0.0003 inches of space. If we could ever build an extremely advanced device to mimic the human eye, the single enormous computer chip would weigh at least 100 pounds, in comparison to the human retina that weighs less than a gram. The retina operates with less than 0.0001 watts of electrical charge. To duplicate the retina's abilities, the imaginary computer would need to consume 300 watts of power. In other words, the retina is 3,000,000 times more efficient in its power consumption.

The wonder of reproduction

When humans engage in sexual intercourse, over 200 million microscopic sperm are released from the male to begin a critical journey lasting between four and six minutes until the potential winners in the race for human life arrive at their goal—the woman's egg, the ova. The woman's reproductive organs have a highly acidic environment to resist harmful bacteria that can cause infection. However, the semen from the husband contains several chemicals as well as the millions of sperm. The husband's Cowper's glands produce several drops of fluid that neutralize the acidity found in the woman's urethral passage to prevent this natural acidity from harming the sperm. Out of the millions that begin the journey, only one sperm out of 200,000 will ever reach the ova, which is the size of half a grain of salt.

Out of the thousand or so potential winners of the race, the Creator has designed us so that only one single sperm will be permitted to penetrate the ova to produce a new baby. The sperm are produced at a rate of approximately sixteen every second, and are produced and stored outside the male torso due to the need to keep the sperm production operating at 96° Fahrenheit, two degrees cooler than the normal body temperature of 98.6. The testicles respond to variations in body and atmospheric temperature by being drawn closer to the torso when it is cool and descending away from the torso when it is too hot to maintain the correct temperature.

As mentioned above, the sperm encounter a very acidic environment to prevent bacteria from damaging her reproductive system. The sperm's head is coated with a protective shield to enable the sperm to survive this hostile acidic environment. The additional components of semen include sugar to provide energy for the sperm's journey. The thousand surviving sperm will meet the ova descending from the woman's ovaries through the fallopian tubes. The ova begins to secrete a special fluid that acts as a chemical homing beacon for the sperm to help them locate their goal. Then the ova releases a special fluid that dissolves the protective shield of the sperm head. Now the uncovered solvent enzymes on the head of the sperm begin their work of dissolving the protective membrane of the ova to allow the sperm to penetrate the ova. The human egg is surrounded by a negative electrical charge, and the sperm is positively charged. Only one sperm will be permitted to drill deep into the ova; no additional sperm will be allowed to continue their attempt to fertilize the ova. At the exact moment of fertilization, when the ova is penetrated by one successful sperm, the ova instantly changes its electrical charge from negative to positive. The two positively-charged bodies, the ova and the other unsuccessful sperm are instantly electrically repelled away from the ova, thus preventing any other sperm from penetrating the ova. *(See picture section, figure 2.)*

Once the one successful sperm penetrates the ova, the DNA in the sperm combine instantly with the DNA of the ova. The combined sperm and ova form the zygote, the first new cell of the future baby, now representing the total genetic combination of the husband and wife—the miracle of a new human life. This remarkable new cell begins instantaneously to divide and grow until a new human being with trillions of cells is born nine months later. The zygote cell will descend through the fallopian tube until it reaches the womb. The zygote cell attaches itself to the wall of the mother's uterus and begins its nine-month growth cycle, living within a marvelous protective fluid known as the amnion liquid, which forms within a special sac in the womb that protects the growing baby from blows or accidents.

When the child is born, the mother's milk includes a remarkable chemical called colostrum. The mother's breasts produce colostrum for the first five days only, to act as a special laxative for the baby to remove the mucus and other harmful waste products that have built up in the newborn's digestive tract. In addition, colostrum contains special antibodies to enhance the baby's immune system during the first vulnerable days of life.

The liver

The Scriptures affirm that the blood is an essential factor in our life. The liver is the essential organ in the body that purifies the bloodstream. Thousands of years ago, Moses wrote these words in the Bible that reveal scientific and medical knowledge far in advance of its day: "For the life of the flesh is in the blood" (Leviticus 17:11). How could Moses have known three thousand years ago what doctors did not know until the discovery, by the English doctor Dr. William Harvey in 1616, of the essential role of the circulation of blood in the function of life. The key to our blood is the purification performed by this marvelous organ—the liver.

The liver is an extraordinarily complex chemical refinery that is a wonder of God's creation. The liver is involved in the essential production of glucose, which forms the main energy that allows our body to function. Our body is constantly exposed to enormous amounts of chemical poisons and harmful waste substances that are naturally produced by our organs and cells in the normal course of our life. Our liver is found on the right side of the upper abdominal cavity, and fulfills its essential function as the primary filter to remove the dangerous toxins from our blood's circulatory system. The role of the kidney is to work in tandem with the liver by removing a variety of water-soluble excess materials and poisons from our body.

The food and drink we consume (meat, potatoes, caffeine, and prescription drugs) would be fatally poisonous to us if it were directly injected into our bloodstream without first being filtered and purified by the liver. After food is digested within the highly acidic fluids of the stomach, it is pumped in squirts into the small intestine, where it is immediately rendered pH neutral by an alkaline solution produced by special glands. Then the still-deadly chemicals in the digested fluid are pumped directly through a special tube into the liver. When this digested fluid arrives, the liver has only ten to twelve seconds to chemically analyze and process the material before it enters the bloodstream. Once the liver has performed its essential function of transforming poisons into harmless material and altering harmful food and drink into nutritious elements, the liver sends the material into the blood system. The blood system will then deliver its vital vitamins, minerals, proteins, new red blood cells, glucose, etc., to the body's sixty trillion cells through seventy-five thousand miles of veins, arteries, and capillaries.

In the liver the blood is warmed up to maintain the precisely required temperature throughout the body. You can travel the globe and sit down in a restaurant to consume a meal of totally unknown food and drink that you have never before experienced. Yet your liver will identify the chemical composition of this unknown material, analyze what chemical reactions and enzymes are needed to neutralize or make nutritious the material needed by your body's trillions of cells, produce these essential chemicals, and perform these complex functions—all in less than twelve seconds. If it couldn't do this, you would die.

The liver also cleans the passing blood from complex surplus and waste materials produced by the trillions of cells, including harmful pharmaceutical residues and excess hormones. In addition, our liver produces the essential globulins, including immune substances and chemical enzymes, to repair our veins. Special Kupffer cells attack harmful bacteria as they pass through the liver in our blood. Additionally, the liver stores up to one liter of our blood supply held in reserve to quickly increase the blood volume in a crisis. Virtually every essential mineral, protein, and a portion of our fat and vitamins are stored within the liver, which communicates to every organ of the body to know when any particular organ of our body needs additional red blood cells, iron, or other proteins.

This essential organ can also repair itself rapidly. Studies have shown that a liver that is two-thirds destroyed can fully repair itself. Astonishingly, the cells in the human liver are capable of performing up to five hundred separate chemical reactions simultaneously. No chemical refinery in the world could hope to match this remarkable production of hundreds of different chemical reactions simultaneously. In addition, the liver can produce up to one thousand essential chemicals, called enzymes, every day as required to instantly chemically alter food, drink, medication, etc., to remove poisons and make food nutritious. If anyone ever demanded that a chemical engineer design and manufacture an enormous chemical refinery covering many acres that could begin to duplicate the functions of the liver, it would be considered absolutely impossible.

The complex "simple cell"

When I hear an atheist speak or write about the evolution of a single living cell as a "simple cell," I am amazed. While most people have assumed that a cell is actually a simple jellylike substance, the truth is that the trillions of cells that form our body and all other live organisms are infinitely more complicated than the most sophisticated and complex supercomputers in existence today.

In 1963, scientists finally penetrated the initial mysteries of the cellular wall and examined the interior of a living cell—what used to be thought of as a very simple biological structure that is the foundation of all biological organisms. The major portion of the cell body was believed to be nothing more than a jelly-like substance that biologists called protoplasm, a term that means "a living substance." However, George Palade, a professor of the Rockefeller Institute in New York, made a remarkable discovery that transformed the science of biology. Dr. Palade discovered an incredibly complex system operating within the cell that is the basis of all forms of life. Palade was amazed to discover an unbelievably intricate and complex system throughout the protoplasm. The scientists identified this internal protoplasm system as the "endoplasmic reticulum." The scientists discovered a remarkable microscopic Universe that involved a massive maze of infinitely microscopic tubes as well as incredibly tiny cells within cells that permeated the complete "simple cell." Many scientists have now acknowledged that the simple cell actually contains the most complex and beautiful system ever found in the whole Universe.

The surface of these incredibly small cells that form our bodies are protected by a membrane that is less than a third of a millionth of an inch thick. Yet the cell wall is remarkably able to control both the entry and exit of thousands of chemicals, enzymes, and proteins that are essential for life to exist. Whenever any one of the sixty trillion cells in our body needs a hormone, an enzyme, a vitamin, a chemical, or a protein, or needs to excrete a harmful waste product, the cell communicates with the rest of our body, and the bloodstream sends its vital fluid through the over seventy-five thousand miles of veins, arteries, and capillaries that reach every single cell of our body to provide essential nutrients and eliminate waste products.

One of the most effective ways to understand the extraordinary complexity of the remarkable functions performed by trillions of these cells is to think of them as a city. These trillions of essential cells perform awesomely complex and intricate functions. These functions include: energy generation; defense against biological invaders; intricate communication links to trillions of other cells simultaneously; sophisticated communication links within and without the cell; transportation systems to move nutritional products within and without the cell; waste disposal systems to eliminate harmful toxins; the generation of energy for all cell functions;

factories capable of generating nutrition from products delivered by the capillaries; defense systems to protect the cell from bacterial and viral invaders; the building of an amazingly successful defense system for the cellular wall; and intricate transportation systems that carry the essential materials into and out of the cell to facilitate life functions.

Essential communication enzymes form on the surface of the microscopic cell to transfer instructions to and from other cells. If a needed nutritional or defensive molecule is available in the passing bloodstream within the thousands of miles of microscopic capillary vessels, the cell literally "reaches out" to engulf it by means of extending a membrane that forms an extending hand that touches and surrounds the necessary material and brings it into the cell.

A human cell is made up of literally thousands of intricate proteins that are absolutely essential for life to continue. These thousands of essential proteins making up our individual cells are themselves indi-vidually composed of over one thousand amino acid molecules, which must be arranged in an amazingly precise sequence that could never have been selected by random chance. Biologists who have examined the details of the "simple cell" have concluded that none of our human cells could ever perform their essential life functions unless every single arrangement and essential function was purposely arranged in the precise pattern that science has finally discovered. These cells can detect the presence of needed molecules, hormones, enzymes, etc., and can instruct the blood to allow these essential nutrients to penetrate the cell when needed while also expelling harmful waste products into the bloodstream to be taken away and eliminated from the body. It is obvious to the scientists that there is a remarkable cooperation and coordination between the thousands of intricate parts of the tiny cells that allow life to function.

Professor Donald Patten wrote, in his book, *The Biblical Flood and the Ice Epoch*, that new discoveries pointed clearly to the fact of Creation:

> It is astonishing to think that this remarkable piece of machinery, which possesses the ultimate capacity to construct every living thing that ever existed on Earth, from giant red wood trees to the human brain, can construct all its own components in a matter of minutes and weigh less than 10^{-16} grams. It is of the order of several thousand million million times smaller than the smallest piece of functional machinery ever constructed by man (until man recently invented nanotechnology).[8]

Human psychology

The book of Proverbs declares that "a merry heart doeth good like a medicine: but a broken spirit drieth the bones" (Proverbs 17:22). While many biblical readers accept this medical advice from the ancient book of Proverbs as a general statement, they would be surprised to learn that modern psychiatry has discovered that good humor and laughter actually improves our overall health. An article in the *Birmingham News* entitled "Laughter: Prescription for Health" confirms the statement found in Proverbs.

The writer declared: "At some point during laughter, your body issues a prescription from the pharmacy in your brain." The article revealed that scientists discovered that the emotion of humor actually triggers the release of specific hormones and chemical endorphins that greatly improve our overall sense of well-being.

Water Lilies

The flowers we encounter everyday when we walk in the city or the country are taken for granted, despite the incredible perfection of their design. Unfortunately, most people fail to recognize the miraculous nature of these flowers because they are so common. If we examine an uncommon and unfamiliar flower from a distant part of the world—the Amazon water lily from the jungles of Brazil—we may awaken to see the evidence and wonder of God's design.

Amazon water lilies first start to grow in the thick mud at the bottom of the Amazon River. However, since these plants require sunlight to live, they quickly begin to grow up to thirty feet toward the surface of the river. When the water lilies finally reach the water's surface, they cease their upward growth and begin to grow round buds with thorns. The buds of the lilies grow into massive leaves on the water's surface, reaching a diameter of up to six feet in as little as a few hours. As the lilies grow to cover the water's surface with very large leaves, they use the sunlight during daylight hours to perform the essential chemical process known as photosynthesis. If the lilies failed to reach the river surface, they would die due to the lack of sunlight and oxygen. Thus, it is vital for the plant's survival that the water float these leaves from these stems that can grow up to thirty-five feet tall and carry the oxygen between the leaves and the roots below.[9] The water lilies curl the brims of their huge leaves upward to prevent them from sinking below the water's surface.

In order to successfully reproduce, the water lilies need the cooperation of another living creature that will carry their pollen from their leaves to another water lily. This reproduction system depends on the actions of a water beetle, which was created by God with a powerful attraction to the color white. Despite an abundance of beautifully multi-colored flowers that are found throughout the Amazon River, these white water lilies exert a compelling attraction to the water beetle that causes these beetles to ignore all other flowers except the white water lily.

When this water beetle lands on the leaf surface, the water lily immediately closes its leaves to imprison the creature for one night, forcing it to become exposed to its pollen. In the morning, the water lily opens its leaves to allow the water beetle to escape to go visit other water lilies and pollinate them. However, the original water lily, having succeeded in transferring its pollen to the beetle, now quickly changes its color to a beautiful pink to prevent that beetle from bringing its own pollen back to it. This remarkable cooperative symbiotic reproductive system involving two species provides compelling evidence of God's intelligent design.

The Bombardier Beetle's Unique Chemical Warfare

The bombardier beetle uses a method of defense that virtually defies belief. It defends itself through an enormously complex defensive system involving the precise use of volatile chemicals. A tremendous amount of research has been completed on the chemical warfare methods used by this beetle to protect itself from its enemies.

Michael J. Behe wrote about the complex defensive strategy utilized by the bombardier beetle in his book, *Darwin's Black Box*, that demonstrated that evolution could never account for the irreducibly complex biological systems we find everywhere in nature. By "irreducibly complex," Behe describes a biological system such as the eye or this beetle's chemical defence system that could never have developed gradually as evolution claims because it won't function at all unless every part of the complex system is present.

This tiny beetle (one half inch) uses a unique defensive system that sends an explosive, scalding hot liquid at its enemy through two specialized secretory lobes that are controlled by the beetle's sphincter muscles. When it senses danger, it squirts two chemicals, hydrogen peroxide and hydroquinone, toward the enemy. In the seconds of buildup to its battle, specialized secretory lobes combine these two chemicals together in a very concentrated mixture. The mixture is initially stored in a storage chamber. This first chamber is connected to another compartment called the explosion chamber. When the insect senses danger, it squeezes the muscles controlling the storage chamber while relaxing the sphincter muscle, allowing the mixture in the storage chamber to transfer to the explosion chamber. Small knobs, known as ectodermal glands, then secrete enzyme catalysts (peroxidase) into the explosive chamber. The key to creating the explosive mixture is the introduction of these enzyme catalysts. In the presence of the catalysts, the hydrogen peroxide quickly decomposes into water and oxygen. The oxygen now reacts with the hydroquinone, producing heat, more water, and the chemical quinone. A large quantity of heat is released and vaporization occurs. The beetle releases boiling hot vapour (100°C) and exploding oxygen out from the exploding chamber through its outlet ducts into the face of its enemy.[10]

Researchers are mystified as to how the beetle can have inside its body a powerful explosive system that provides no protection at all until all of the other parts of the system are also in place. The defensive system of the bombardier beetle totally refutes the theory of evolution because this system is irreducibly complex. The entire system is absolutely useless to protect the beetle until every part of the complex storage and explosive chambers, exploding chemicals, the enzyme catalysts, and chemical inhibitors are in place.

In other words, the entire system is useless and provides no evolutionary survival advantage until every part of this remarkably complex system is in place. No evolutionist can explain the procedure by which random mutation and natural selection could ever have formed this unique form of complex chemical warfare. Random mutation changes would not provide any advantage and thus would not be passed on to future generations. Until every single part of this system is in place, the beetle is without defenses. The only logical conclusion is that this complex chemical weapons system was intelligently designed by the Creator and was given to the beetle from the very beginning.

Cuckoo Birds

The cuckoo bird has one of the oddest reproductive strategies to be found in nature. Rather than face the rather arduous parenting, nesting, and feeding requirements necessitated by laying twenty eggs every reproductive season, the cuckoo bird utilizes a remarkable strategy: it gets birds from other species to incubate, feed, and care for each of its twenty offspring—and it does this without the other bird species even knowing that they have adopted the cuckoo's eggs to raise as their own.

This unusual system works as follows. When the cuckoo is getting ready to lay the first of its twenty eggs (it lays one egg every second day), it scouts out its neighborhood to discover the nests of twenty other birds of a wide variety of species that happen to be building nests in preparation for laying their own eggs. When the cuckoo is ready to lay its first egg, it watches in secret for a neighboring bird such as a robin to lay several eggs in its nest. The moment the robin parents leave their recently-laid eggs to gather more material for the nest and food for their chicks that should be hatched shortly, the cuckoo swoops down on the robin's nest and lays its first egg in the nest. Before leaving, the cuckoo carefully ejects one of the robins' eggs from the nest to confuse the returning parents. Though the new cuckoo egg will differ in smell, size, and color from the missing egg, the robin parents will accept that the cuckoo egg is theirs because the correct number of eggs is still present. The cuckoo mother never returns to check up on her orphaned egg. *(See picture section, figure 3.)*

When the adopted cuckoo egg hatches, the robins will feed the new cuckoo chick as if it were their own. However, as soon as the robin parents leave the nest for the first time to acquire more food, the cuckoo chick throws the remaining robin eggs out of the nest. When the robins return, they are surprised to find only one bird in the nest—the cuckoo. Since there is only one chick to feed, the robins will now devote their complete parenting efforts to feed the one surviving offspring, even though it is not their own kin. Through this remarkably selfish but effective technique, the cuckoo bird arranges for twenty other pairs of parenting birds from a number of different species to care for each of her twenty eggs. It is not unusual to find smaller birds such a chickadees caring for and feeding a newborn cuckoo chick, which is already much larger than themselves.

How does the newborn cuckoo chick know how to maximize its survival chances by knocking the other eggs out of the nest so that it is the only chick left to feed? How does the adult cuckoo know to spy out twenty other birds getting ready to lay eggs and lay its own egg in their nest after knocking out one of the original eggs—especially in light of the fact that the cuckoo chick is never parented by its mother?

Beaver

When I spent my summers growing up at our ranch in Canada, I had numerous opportunities to observe the wonders of God's creation in the stars as well as the tremendous variety of animals to be found in the northern forests of North America. Of all of the animals that I enjoyed observing, the beaver was one of the most fascinating because it is truly a hydrological engineer second to none in its ability to control water levels in its environment and to build and repair complex dams. Beavers need to create a stationary pool of water to a precise depth to provide a livable home and defensible place to reproduce and protect their young offspring.

In order to create a stationary pond, the beaver finds an active stream surrounded by higher ground. Then it builds a dam that blocks the water flow until a sufficient amount of water accumulates to form a large, still water pool, usually three to six feet deep, where the beaver can safely build its nest. It is remarkable that all beaver dams are constructed at an angle of forty-five degrees, the same precise angle that is followed by all hydroelectric dams throughout the world today. However, the beavers were the first to use this design. This angle has been determined to be the most efficient and effective design to hold back the massive water pressure in a dam. In addition, these beavers construct the dam using special channels that allow excess water to run off, maintaining the required water level but allowing the stream to continue past its dam.

The beaver was given a unique set of teeth by the Creator to construct these essential dams. The beaver has a remarkable set of front teeth that it uses to nibble the trees, and they continue to grow throughout the life of the beaver. Remarkably, the size of the beaver's back teeth remains constant throughout its life and will not continue to grow to a harmful size. Meanwhile, the four front teeth that constantly erode and chip away are constantly replaced throughout its life. How can anyone who honestly contemplates the life of the beaver fail to recognize that its life and the design of its dams reflect the divine instructions from a Creator?

Occasionally, the beaver will choose to build its dam and resulting pond in a place that blocks an essential path used by a rancher to move livestock. Then a battle of wills begins as to whether the rancher's destruction of the dam will succeed over the beaver's rebuilding efforts throughout the following night. Usually the beaver wins.

Honeybees

The honeybee is an absolute wonder of God's Creation. Bees construct their hive into a complex honeycomb structure using beeswax produced from their own bodies to house a colony of up to 75,000 insects. All honeycombs found in the hive and in all hives throughout the world are constructed to the same precise engineering specifications. The hexagonal structure of the honeycomb has intrigued scientists for a century because mathematicians have calculated that it is the best possible geometric structure to maximize storage. It is the most efficient storage structure possible and uses the least amount of beeswax in its construction because each cell utilizes the walls of surrounding cells.

The honeycomb is constructed with cells inclined precisely thirteen degrees on two sides to prevent the honey from escaping the mouth of the cell. One of the most astonishing aspects of a hive is that the tens of thousands of worker bees simultaneously begin construction of their hive from three different starting points and directions. The completed hive has thousands of individual cells that are precisely joined together with hundreds of separate angles, forming a perfectly engineered hexagonal comb structure that rivals anything produced by computers and human engineers. To have the final structure so perfectly engineered, the bees would have to know at the very beginning and throughout construction the precise distances between each starting point, and adjust the construction accordingly. However, it would take a computer to do the calculations. Engineers have wondered how the bees can possibly accomplish this marvel of construction. The only logical conclusion is that the tens of thousands of bees are receiving instructions from a single source—the Creator. *(See picture section, figure 4.)*

The social organization of the bee colony involves different groups of bees following entirely different duties to serve the hive. One group of worker bees stays at the entrance and fans their wings to ventilate the hive and maintain the proper humidity and keep the temperature at precisely 95°F. If the hive temperature rises or lowers more than a few degrees, the precious honey will spoil and lose its nutritional qualities. Some worker bees are tasked with protecting the hive from contamination from harmful bacteria or other insects. As soon as the guardian bees detect a problem, they alert the rest of the hive to begin a mass attack on the intruder. If any intruder actually succeeds in getting into the hive and is too large to remove, the worker bees actually embalm the object with their very effective antibacterial bee resin (propolis) to protect the integrity of the colony.

The bees collect flower nectar during the summer months and combine this with chemicals secreted from their body to produce honey, one of the most perfect foods on Earth. The bee marks the flower that it has visited with a small drop of scent that tells every other bee to ignore it, as the pollen is already consumed. This unusual action is very efficient because it saves other bees from wasting time on an empty flower.

The bee locates pollen from flowers in an area up to half a mile from the hive. The bee that finds the flowers returns to the hive to let its fellow workers know precisely where they must fly to locate the food source. Incredibly, rather than lead the others back, the bee instructs the other bees where to find the pollen through the means of a very complex dance. Biologists have determined that the precise information regarding the direction, distance, and amount of pollen is conveyed to the other bees through a repeated zigzag dance following a figure-8 pattern. The precise line between the Sun's position and the hive and the angle between the zigzags of the dancing bee provides the exact location of the food source. Other body movements include wagging its bottom and producing air currents through wing movements. For example, to communicate to the other bees that the pollen is located five hundred yards from the hive, the bee will wag the bottom of its body twenty times per minute.

There is an apparent problem in providing precise orientation to the other bees in that, during the time taken by the bee to fly home to the hive, the Sun's position keeps changing. Every four minutes the Sun moves one degree of longitude. However, the bee has remarkable eyes composed of hundreds of microscopic hexagonal lenses that focus on a narrow beam enabling the bee to identify the Sun's position based on the time of day. As the minutes pass, the bee alters its precise dance to adjust its instructions to compensate for the Sun's movement. Experiments that upset the bee's time sense by altering its internal clock with artificial light changes proved that this also interfered with its ability to calculate the Sun's correct position. Only the Creator could have formed such a masterpiece of engineering.

God's gift to mankind, honey, is one of the most complex foods produced in nature. The primary components of honey are sugars including fructose and glucose. It also contains vitamins B_1, B_2, B_3, B_5, B_6, and C, as well as minerals including calcium, sodium, chlorine, sulfur phosphate, magnesium, potassium, and iron. The products of the honeybee are remarkable in their nutritional and disease-fighting powers. It is well known that honey, bee resin, and royal jelly are all extremely helpful in the cure of many diseases.

It is very unusual that the bees that use honey for a food source for the bee colony during the cold months of winter actually produce a great abundance of honey, far beyond their own needs. Why? It appears that this overproduction is part of the Creator's plan to provide a perfect food source for humanity. This phenomenon of over production beyond the species own needs is also seen in cows that produce amounts of milk far beyond that needed for its calves. We also see this in chickens, which daily lay eggs.

Monarch Butterflies

Monarch butterflies are among the most gloriously beautiful and ingenious of the millions of insects who migrate across great distances in the course of their lives. However, the life and migration pattern of the monarch butterfly is significantly more complex than that of most other birds, fish, or insects.

There are four generations of butterflies in the course of a year. The first three generations of butterflies only live for up to six weeks from the time they develop out of the caterpillar stage till death. During the annual cycle of the monarch, three separate generations live their short lives in Canada during the spring and summer months. *(See picture section, figure 5.)*

The fourth generation that will migrate from Canada three thousand miles south to the mountainous plateaus of Mexico and home again are born in the late summer and will live for eight months. Hundreds of millions of monarchs from across Canada begin their remarkable, 3,000-mile-long migration on the night of the autumn equinox—September 21—when the amount of day is precisely balanced by the amount of night. The monarchs finally arrive in Mexico on the plateaus and ridges of volcanic mountains almost two miles above sea level. These butterflies now survive on water alone for four months, from December till March. When their fast ends toward the middle of March, the monarchs begin to feast on the abundant nectar of the tremendous number of flowers available on the mountains, building the fuel reserves they will need for the long flight ahead. The butterflies will mate in the middle of March just before setting out on their extraordinary migration back to Canada.

On the night of the spring equinox—March 21—the enormous colony of millions of monarch butterflies ascends from its southern Mexican home into the heavens to begin the epic migration back to Canada. When it arrives back in Canada, the whole generation of monarchs give birth to the next generation of their species. Then the complete fourth generation of butterflies dies. The new first generation of the new cycle born in Canada will live six weeks. This will be followed by the second and third generations, each of which will live only approximately six weeks.

This remarkable situation raises a number of questions: How can the genetic code of the monarch instruct the fourth generation to live over six months longer than the other three short-lived generations? How can the fourth-generation monarchs know to migrate three thousand miles to arrive at a plateau in Mexico when the other three short-lived generations do not have these DNA migration instructions? How could an evolutionist ever explain how the fourth generation knows to begin its long southern migration on the night of the autumnal equinox and to begin its northern migration on the night of the spring equinox? The only reasonable explanation is that the Creator has programmed the beautiful monarchs to follow these precise instructions since their original creation.

Pepsis Wasps

The giant wasp, often called pepsis, utilizes one of the most unusual reproductive strategies. Unlike most other wasps and insects, the pepsis doesn't build a nest to incubate its eggs. The pepsis uses its sensitive sensors as it walks along the desert sand detecting the scent of the poisonous tarantula. After detecting the tunnel used by a tarantula, the wasp approaches and then attacks the much larger spider. The tarantula bites the wasp and injects its deadly poison. However, the wasp has a unique antidote to tarantula poison in its bloodstream that totally protects it during the attack.

The second stage of the battle is joined when the wasp uses its long stinger to inject its own venom into the upper left portion of the tarantula's stomach, the spider's most vulnerable part. Instead of killing the spider, the venom paralyzes the tarantula. Now the wasp drags the paralyzed spider back to a hole it has just dug for this purpose. After placing the paralyzed spider on its back in the hole, the wasp creates a hole in the spider's stomach and deposits one egg into it. In a matter of a few days the egg will incubate and produce a pepsis stage of the wasp that will consume the paralyzed tarantula's body for food and shelter until it develops into a full adult. Remarkably, the wasp will repeat this procedure twenty times over the following days until twenty wasp eggs are growing inside the bodies of twenty deadly, but paralyzed, tarantulas. It defies understanding to imagine how such an incredibly complex reproductive strategy involving two different species could have developed through random mutations, especially the development of a special antidote to tarantula poison in the bloodstream of the wasp.

Penguins

The life and reproductive cycle of the Antarctic penguin is quite unusual. The temperature in the Antarctic can drop below −40°F. The penguins are protected from the extreme cold by a very thick layer of body fat and by a quite high body temperature of 104 degrees. The female lays her one egg as much as sixty miles from the ocean, which is the only possible source of food. Once the egg is laid, the female almost immediately leaves the nest and travels the long journey to the ocean to begin a vigorous hunting and feeding cycle for the next four months. The father penguin has the sole job of incubating and protecting the egg. For four months the male penguin remains with the egg, protecting it from the sixty miles per hour polar winds without any food, as he cannot travel to the sea to feed himself. During the four month fast, the father loses up to fifty percent of his entire weight.

At the precise time the egg finally cracks open, the well-fed mother returns from the sea to locate her mate and provide her newborn penguin with the essential food she had stored during her hunting period.

Rattlesnakes

The rattlesnake has an extremely sensitive and complex system that enables it to detect the slightest change in temperature in its environment. Heat-detecting organs located in the snake's head can sense its prey or another predator from a distance through the raised temperature emitted by the other animal's body. A temperature change as small as one-thirtieth of a degree Fahrenheit can be detected by the rattlesnake. The snake's forked tongue can also detect its prey from the extremely faint odors emitted by animals in its immediate vicinity in total darkness.

When the rattlesnake detects its prey, it approaches as close as possible, coils its body, and strikes at an incredible speed of almost fifty miles a second (180,000 miles per hour). The snake's inch-long fangs are connected to glands in its head that contain poisonous venom that it injects into its prey with great force by squeezing the muscles surrounding the venom glands. Rattlesnake venom is so poisonous that a fraction of an ounce of venom could kill a quarter of a million rats. The snake's venom is one of the most complex materials in nature, with over fifty different chemical components. It kills its prey by immediately paralyzing the central nervous system or through coagulation of the prey's blood. The unique jaw structure of the rattlesnake allows it to open its jaw a full 180 degrees to enable it to swallow its paralyzed prey, even though the prey is larger than the snake's head.

It is incomprehensible how such intricate and efficient defensive and predatory organs and complex venom could have developed in the rattlesnake by random mutation, as evolutionists suggest. The snake's defence system includes the amazingly complex venom, the venom glands to hold it, the surrounding muscles to contract and expel the poison, and hollow fangs to deliver the venom. This entire system does not work at all unless every single one of the essential subsystems is present and operating with full efficiency. Yet the theory of evolution imagines that extremely small accidental mutations persist and are retained because they offer some survival advantage. But the rattlesnake illustrates the virtually universal situation found in nature of irreducibly complex systems that require all parts to be in place in order for it to function at all.

Bats

Bats live in dark places such as caves, barns, and attics. They fly at night to acquire the insects needed for their food requirements. The bat's eyesight is weak. However, God provided the bat with an extremely sophisticated and complex sonar echo-location system that emits ultra-high-frequency sound waves—ultrasound—at more than twenty thousand cycles per second. The high frequency of these ultrasounds makes them undetectable by humans, who have a more limited sound range. However, the sound waves hit and reflect back from any surrounding objects—the ground, trees, humans, walls, bats, and the insects they hunt. Remarkably, the bat's brain is able to form a three-dimensional matrix of its environment based on the reflected sound waves to precisely determine the distance and direction of the surrounding objects. The detailed information facilitates the incredible accuracy of the bat's flight and capture of insects in the dark.

The evolutionists can never adequately explain how a tremendously sophisticated echo-location navigation system such as the bat's sonar system, more sophisticated than World War II military sonar systems, could ever have developed through natural selection and random mutation. The evolutionist's problem of explaining sonar as the result of accidental mutation becomes even more impossible when you consider the fact that two entirely unrelated species—the dolphin and the toothed whale—also possess a similar underwater sonar system.

Dolphins

The dolphin uses a specialized organ in the front of its skull that produces ultrasonic underwater high-frequency sound waves (200,000 vibrations per second—ten times the frequency of the bat's sonar system). The brain of the dolphin instantaneously calculates the nature of its surrounding environment from the reverberations from these reflected ultrasounds. No one can rationally conclude that the system of echo-location sonar could ever develop by accidental mutation in three totally unconnected species such as bats, dolphins, and the toothed whale. It is suggestive of the true divinely-created nature of our Universe and life itself that it is only in the last century that scientists could develop the sophisticated technology to mimic this sonar directional guidance of bats, toothed whales, and dolphins in our billion-dollar submarines. Such a complex system could never have been formed by chance.

Another interesting aspect of the dolphin is that it's very high speed in swimming is accentuated by the curious shape of the snout on the very front of its head. Many experiments by the U.S. Navy revealed that the design of the dolphin's snout was very purposeful in that it cuts through the water much more efficiently than any other shape found in the heads of marine animals. However, the remarkably efficient snout of the dolphin can be no accident of evolution. It is definitely the result of divine design. When marine engineers charged with designing the great supertankers that traverse the oceans considered the problems of fuel efficiency and water resistance, they wondered why the dolphin, with its unusual snout, could swim so quickly that it could almost effortlessly keep pace with the fastest tankers and navy warships powered by enormous nuclear reactors. They completed a sophisticated computer analysis on the effect of the dolphin's snout shape on minimizing the huge water friction.

The result of incorporating the Creator's design of the dolphin's snout into modern supertankers and military vessels has been to cut the water's resistance more efficiently than any other design. The new dolphin design on modern supertankers has produced a saving of up to 25 percent of the enormous amount of fuel used in each journey of these great ships. This innovation derived from God's creation has resulted in a very significant savings for the oil tanker companies throughout the world. *(See picture section, figure 6.)*

There is another aspect of God's superb creation of the

incredibly fast dolphins that had a profound influence on the development of modern submarine technology. The dolphin's skin consists of three specialized layers. The outermost layer is both flexible and extremely thin. The middle skin layer is composed of a compressible sponge-type material that is capable of transmitting to the innermost skin layer any sudden pressures from a changed environment or shift in direction. The inner skin layer is quite thick and is composed of flexible hairlike material, similar to a comb.

The German navy examined the dolphin's skin and began to create a duplication using modern materials to mimic the dolphin's remarkable skin. Finally, the German naval engineers announced they had duplicated the dolphin's skin characteristics with a synthetic coating composed of two specialized rubber layers separated by a material composed of bubbles that resembled the characteristics of the dolphin's skin. The result was a remarkable 250 percent increase in the speed of the submarine as it traveled beneath the ocean's surface. In the distant past, the Creator had provided the best possible solution for accelerating speed underwater. Who can honestly contemplate these discoveries without concluding that all we observe in nature is overwhelming evidence for the existence of a divine Intelligence that created the vast number of creatures according to His purpose?

Geckos

The gecko is a very small tropical lizard that displays a seemingly miraculous ability to walk up vertical walls and even walk upside down across ceilings with perfectly smooth surfaces. An article in the science journal *Nature* described a study by scientists who tried to determine how geckos can stick to such smooth surfaces when the studies show that there is no evidence that it uses any glue-like material or suction device. Remarkably, the biologists found that millions of microscopic hairs, or setae, on the tiny toes of the gecko are actually so small that they can directly attach themselves to the individual molecules forming the surface of the plaster in the walls and ceiling, or even a perfectly smooth surface such as a glass window.

The gecko's toe's strong adhesion to the surface molecules of the wall or ceiling is effected through a scientific force that acts between individual atoms known as the Van der Waals force (named after its nineteenth-century Dutch discover). The gecko's microscopic foot hairs split and thus allow up to a billion tiny spatulae to come into close contact with the surface molecules, creating a strong adhesive force. The adhesive power of this system is so strong that a gecko can hang its entire body weight with only a single toe touching the ceiling. One single seta has enough adhesive power to support the weight of an ant. It has been calculated that one million gecko's setae, which would only cover a dime, could support the weight of a 45-pound child. If it were possible to engage all of a gecko's setae at one time, the adhesion could support a 280-pound man.[11]

Hummingbirds

The smallest bird in the world is the hummingbird, which is a marvel of aerodynamic engineering. Its small wings beat up to eighty strokes every single second. Although the hummingbird weighs only one-tenth of an ounce, its aerodynamic abilities to fly forward, backward, sideways, and to hover in one spot for minutes is unrivalled. The tiny hummingbird's heart beats over a thousand times a minute, creating an awesome metabolic rate that requires virtually non-stop feeding to support its energy output.

The nectar of flowers, which is mostly high-energy sugar, provides the primary food for hummingbirds as the bird draws over a dozen sips of nectar every second. In light of the fact that there is no other bird that has ever existed on Earth that remotely resembles the extraordinary aerodynamic system of the hummingbird, it is apparent that this tiny marvel of engineering provides compelling proof of God's intelligent design.

Scientists have calculated that the tiny hummingbird will beat its wings more than two and a half million times during its 1,800-mile migration between Alaska and Hawaii. The enormous expenditure of energy as the bird flies up to fifty miles a day causes its internal temperature to rise to as high as 143°F! Hummingbirds actually slow down their metabolism and hybernate every night in order to conserve energy. Some hummingbirds can fly as long as thirty-six hours without stopping to rest. No one who contemplates the extraordinary design of the hummingbird can honestly conclude that anything that is engineered with such extraordinary precision could ever have developed as the result of evolution's blind mutations.

Canada Geese

Everyone in North America has watched with wonder as thousands of Canada geese migrate north and south every year. We watch these magnificent birds join in flocks to form a V-shaped configuration. Scientists have now determined that the V shape is no accident. The leader of the formation flies in the lead position at the center of the V. As the strongest bird in the flock, the leader uses his superior strength to shield the following birds from the opposing air currents, and provides a significant lift force for the birds that fly behind him in the formation. Aeronautical engineers have calculated that the entire flock gains an improved energy efficiency and speed of up to 23 percent by using this formation. Could these geese have discovered this improvement alone? *(See picture section, figure 8.)*

Electrical Fish

One of the most astonishing biological systems is found in the South American and African electric fish. On opposite sides of the world, we find two species of fish that are able to "see" in the darkest water through generating an electrostatic field in the surrounding murky water. These two species are able to detect their prey and other predators by measuring the distortion of the electrostatic field in the water caused by the presence of their bodies.

Another fascinating example is the ability of several separate aquatic species to generate a high-voltage electrical charge that they discharge through the water to kill their prey. Remarkably, this highly sophisticated system involving the purposeful discharge of an electrical bolt is found in totally unrelated species such as stingrays, torpedo rays, electric catfish, and electric eels in different parts of the world.

Woodpeckers

Our Creator's providential design is revealed in the woodpecker that is familiar to all North Americans. A beautiful woodpecker often appears only a few feet outside my library window, searching for insects beneath the bark of the trees in my backyard. The woodpecker has two toes in front and two toes in the rear of its feet, allowing it to grip the vertical trunk of a tree quite firmly with its unusually strong legs while pecking up to one hundred times a minute through bark for insects.

While the bills of all other birds are directly connected to their skull, the woodpecker is unique in that it has unusual spongy tissue between its bill and skull. This spongy tissue acts as a protective shock-absorber to cushion its brain from damage while it pecks forcefully at a tree trunk for several hours. It is not unusual for a woodpecker to actually peck through solid concrete in its quest for insects or in the act of burying seeds for future food. It has extremely sensitive hearing and a powerful sense of smell to detect its insect prey, which may be hidden under an inch of bark.

The woodpecker uses its short tail-feathers as support to brace its body against the tree trunk while it pecks searching for food. After the bird either bores a hole or locates a small tunnel bored through the bark by an insect, the woodpecker inserts its extremely long tongue into the narrow tunnel until it reaches the insect. The tongue of a woodpecker is unique in that it is not attached to the rear of its mouth, as it would be in any other species of bird. The woodpecker's tongue is five inches in length (up to four times longer than its beak) and it is coiled around its brain within its skull, allowing the bird to capture its insect prey deep within the tree trunk.

Gray Sea Slugs

Another wonder of creation is the nudibranch sea slug, which utilizes the most astonishing defense system I have ever seen. Although sea anemones are quite unattractive to almost all fish and crabs in the ocean because they use a very unpleasant but highly effective poisoned venom to defend itself, the gray sea slug feeds exclusively on sea anemones. The anemones are not plants, but actually predatory animals with tentacles on their backs and sides that contain barbed poisoned sting arrows that can be instantly fired at a predator from coiled hollow tubes or filaments. The sea anemones use these poison darts to attack small organisms, to defend against large predators, and to fight battles for territory with other anemones. These tiny poisoned darts are probably the fastest defense response in any animal species. At the slightest touch or pressure from a fish, crab, or scuba diver, the poison capsule turns inside out and drives the venom-filled tube into its prey, causing enormous pain or death.

While other aquatic creatures wisely avoid encounters with anemones, the gray sea slug actually makes these dangerous creatures the main source of its food. Somehow, the sea slug is able to tear apart the dangerous anemone and swallow its poisoned darts without triggering the explosion of venom. However, while digesting the body of the anemone, the tubes holding the loaded poisoned darts are not consumed inside the sea slug's stomach. Instead, the gray sea slug is able to load these highly reactive tubes and their poisoned darts into a series of tiny tubes that extend from the sea slug's stomach right through its body to the very tips on the tentacles or spurs on the sea slug's back and sides. It is remarkable that the sea slug stores these deadly poisoned darts grown by another animal species as its own new missile-firing chemical weapons system. When a predator approaches the sea slug, it fires the exploding poisonous missiles out of its tentacles to attack its enemy.

No evolutionary scientist could ever create a realistic scenario whereby the sea slug could ever have gradually developed such an unusual defense system through gradual mutations over tens of thousands of generations. This symbiotic defensive system involving one animal species, the gray sea slug, using the complex defensive weaponry of another animal species, the anemone, is extraordinary evidence of God's intelligent design.

Notes

1. *ABC's of the Human Body*, Readers Digest Press, 1987, p. 5.
2. Isaac Asimov, "In the Game of Energy and Thermodynamics You Can't Even Break Even," *Smithsonian* (June 1970), p. 10.
3. Fred Hoyle and Chandra Wickramasinghe, *Evolution from Space*, London: J. M. Dent and Sons Co., 1981, p. 330.
4. Charles Darwin, *The Origin of Species*, New York: Avenel Books, 1979, p. 217.
5. Charles Darwin, letter to Asa Gray, F. Darwin, ed., *Life and Letters of Charles Darwin*, vol. 2, London: John Murray, 1883, p. 273.
6. E. Mayer, *Systematics and the Origin of Species*. N.Y. Columbia: University Press, 1942, p. 296.
7. John Stevens, *Byte*, April 1985.
8. Donald Patten, *The Biblical Flood and the Ice Epoch*, Seattle: Pacific Meridian, 1996, pp. 194–224.
9. David Attenborough, *The Private Life of Plants*, Princeton University Press, 1995, p. 291.
10. Michael J. Belie, *Darwin's Black Box*, New York: Free Press, 1996, pp. 32–33.
11. "How Geckos Stick, Secrets to Making Gecko Glue Unlocked," *Lewis & Clark College*, August 27, 2002, Web site: http://www.newswise.com/articles/2002/8/GECKOS.LCC.html

3

Astronomy Reveals the Intelligent Design of the Universe

Thou, even thou, art Lord alone; thou hast made heaven, the heaven of heavens, with all their host, the Earth, and all things that are therein, the seas, and all that is therein, and thou preservest them all; and the host of heaven worshippeth thee (Nehemiah 9:6).

The heavens declare the glory of God; and the firmament sheweth his handywork. Day unto day uttereth speech, and night unto night sheweth knowledge (Psalm 19:1-2).

O Lord our Lord, how excellent is thy name in all the Earth! who hast set thy glory above the heavens. . . . When I consider thy heavens, the work of thy fingers, the moon and the stars, which thou hast ordained; What is man, that thou art mindful of him? and the son of man, that thou visitest him? For thou hast made him a little lower than the angels, and hast crowned him with glory and honour. Thou madest him to have dominion over the works of thy hands: thou hast put all things under his feet (Psalm 8:1, 3-6).

God: The First Cause of the Universe

The laws of logic demand that every known effect must result from a previous cause. The ancient Romans created a maxim that included the natural conclusion of logic, *Ex nihilo nihil fit:* "Nothing comes from nothing." The Universe must have been created by God—an eternal supernatural being existing outside both time and space. Everything that exists must be the result of a previous cause. It is obvious to any serious thinking person that there cannot be an infinite series of causes. Initially, logic demands that there must have been a First Cause. The First Cause itself was not caused by anything else. That First Cause, by logical necessity, is God, who exists eternally outside of time and the Universe. Atheists sometimes ask: Then who created God? The answer is that no one created God. God is an uncreated eternal Being outside time and space, without a beginning or end.

Lift up your eyes on high, and behold who hath

created these things, that bringeth out their host by number: he calleth them all by names by the greatness of his might, for that he is strong in power; not one faileth (Isaiah 40:26).

Evidence for Creation

A famous existential philosopher, Professor Martin Heidegger, once wrote, "Why is there any Being at all, why not far rather, Nothing?" When we examine the extraordinary factors that combine together in the most remarkable manner to allow both the Universe and the glory of Creation—humanity—to exist and flourish, we stand in awe as we contemplate the beautiful and marvelous creation that it is our privilege to live in.

Scientific discoveries made during the 1920s and 30s transformed modern astronomers' understanding of the basic structure and form of the Universe. Until that point in time, virtually all astronomers believed that science had established that the Universe was static; the steady state Universe had existed forever. They concluded, naturally, that if the Universe had always existed, if it was never created, then there was no need for a Creator.

The French philosopher George Politzer expressed the almost universal prevailing opinion held by intellectuals that the Universe had always existed:

The Universe was not a created object. . . . If it were, then it would have to be created instantaneously by God and brought into existence from nothing. To admit creation, one has to admit, in the first place, the existence of a moment when the Universe did not exist, and that something came out of nothingness. This is something to which science cannot accede.[1]

However, many scientists, such as Sir Arthur Eddington, discovered that Professor Albert Einstein's brilliant mathematical field equations established conclusively that the Universe could not have existed infinitely. Professor Eddington admitted, in his book, *Cosmos and Creator*, that the idea of Creation deeply troubled him. "Philosophically, the notion of a beginning of the present order of Nature is repugnant to me."[2] However, Eddington acknowledged that the discovery of the Universe's creation eliminated a huge barrier to faith.

It will perhaps be said that the conclusion to be drawn from these arguments from modern science, is that religion first became possible for a reasonable scientific man about the year 1927.[3]

These new discoveries produced a revolution in scientific thought as scientists struggled to adapt to this new radical truth that upset all of their previous assumptions. Obviously, if the Universe had a definite beginning in time, then it is essential that there must be a Creator who stands outside this Universe. A Universe that springs into existence together with time, space, energy, and mass is obviously a Universe that does not agree with the philosophy of either pantheism or atheism.

The year 1927 marked a significant milestone in the advancement of our scientific knowledge of our Universe's origin. The brilliant American astronomer Edwin Hubble used the new Hooker telescope at

Mount Wilson in California to discover that the distant light sources he observed were not individual stars but were actually astronomical phenomena called nebulae. They were far distant galaxies, each containing untold billions of stars like our own home galaxy, the Milky Way. Remarkably, Dr. Hubble discovered that these enormous galaxies were actually moving away from our galaxy and from each other at stupendous velocities. Even more surprising, the astronomer found that those galaxies furthest from our own were moving away from us with even greater velocity than nearby galaxies.

After Dr. Albert Einstein had personally verified, through Sir Edwin Hubble's enormous 100-inch-wide telescope at Mount Wilson, that the galaxies were indeed expanding away from us at tremendous velocities, he realized that the Universe must logically have had a definite beginning at some point in the distant past. Einstein later acknowledged in his writing that the Universe definitely had a beginning. Professor Einstein later wrote that he wanted

> to know how God created the world. I am not interested in this or that phenomenon, in the spectrum of this or that element. I want to know His thoughts, the rest are details.[4]

The brilliant seventeenth-century scientist, Sir Isaac Newton, wrote in his book *Observations on Daniel and the Revelation of St. John:* "The most beautiful system of the Sun, planets and comets could only proceed from the counsel and dominion of an intelligent and powerful Being." Four hundred years ago, Newton stated that the Creator had placed the stars "at immense distances from one another." He acknowledged that the "diversity of natural things" could never have been produced by "blind metaphysical necessity," but only by an intelligent supernatural Creator."

Newton wrote that "blind fate" couldn't possibly account for the "wonderful Uniformity" that was demonstrated by the planetary movements. "Gravity may put the planets in motion, but without the divine power it could never put them into such a circulating motion as they have."[5]

An Extraordinary Balance Between the Universe's Rate of Expansion and Collapse

At the moment of Creation, God caused the Universe—including time, space, matter, and energy—to begin expanding at an extraordinary speed, which continues today. The force of the gravitation He created was, and still is, precisely balanced with marvelous precision to match exactly the Universe's powerful expansion force. The Creator used the force of gravity to cause matter to combine together to form galaxies and stars, while the expansion of space caused the Universe to continue to grow in size and not collapse back upon itself. If the expansion force and speed were even slightly stronger, no stars or galaxies would have been able to stabilize, and our solar system would not exist. However, if the expansion speed were even a fraction weaker, then the Universe would have collapsed upon itself. It is important to realize that it is space itself that is expanding, carrying with it the galaxies and stars.

How, precisely, did the expansion speed of the

expanding space need to be balanced against the force of gravity? These two fundamental forces needed to be balanced to an absolutely astonishing level of precision that totally defies the odds of probability. Even Dr. Stephen Hawking, although an agnostic, admitted that it was incomprehensible that the Universe that exists today could ever have formed by random chance:

> Why did the Universe start out with so nearly the critical rate of expansion that separates models [of the Universe] that recollapse from those that go on expanding forever, so that even now, ten thousand million years later, it is still expanding at nearly the critical rate? If the rate of expansion one second after the Big Bang had been smaller by even one part in a hundred thousand million million, the Universe would have recollapsed before it ever reached its present state.[6]

Professor Lawrence Henderson of Harvard University acknowledged that scientific evidence confirms that our solar system was endowed with unique characteristics that prepared it to be a habitable environment for living organisms, including human life.

> The great difficulty appears to be that there is here no possibility of interaction. In our solar system, at least, the fitness of the environment far precedes the existence of the living organisms.[7]

In other words, there is no rational, credible, materialistic explanation for the fact that our solar system, and Earth itself, are uniquely fitted to accommodate human life unless God created all of this Universe according to

His divine Purpose as the Scriptures declare: "The Earth hath he given to the children of men" (Psalm 115:16).

A NASA astronomer, John O'Keefe, wrote about the remarkable nature of the Universe:

We are, by astronomical standards, a pampered, cosseted, cherished group of creatures. . . . If the Universe had not been made with the most exacting precision we could never have come into existence. It is my view that these circumstances indicate the Universe was created for man to live in.[8]

The astronomer Dr. Hugh Ross, wrote:

If time's beginning is concurrent with the beginning of the Universe, as the space-theorem says, then the cause of the Universe must be some entity operating in a time dimension completely independent of and pre-existent to the time dimension of cosmos. This conclusion is powerfully important to our understanding of who God is and who or what God isn't. It tells us that God is not the Universe itself, nor is God contained within the Universe.[9]

This is a powerful refutation of the New Age pantheism that imagines God is the Universe.

Significantly, Sir Fred Hoyle wrote that the idea of an unplanned accidental so-called "Big Bang" explosion producing order is nonsense. What he is saying is that explosions produce disorder. However, Creation produced the most precise and complex development of a Universe of astonishingly intricate designs that our scientists are only now discovering. The odds against our Universe, our Earth, and humanity itself occurring as a result of a chance explosion without a supernatural Designer are zero.

The big bang theory holds that the Universe began with a single explosion. Yet as can be seen below, an explosion merely throws matter apart, while the big bang has mysteriously produced the opposite effect—with matter clumping together in the form of galaxies.[10]

The "fine-tuning" of the Universe

Paul Davies, a respected professor of theoretical physics, calculated how fine-tuned the speed of expansion after the initial moment of Creation was, and he reached a remarkable conclusion:

Careful measurement puts the rate of expansion very close to a critical value at which the Universe will just escape its own gravity and expand forever. A little slower and the cosmos would collapse, a little faster and the cosmic material would have long ago completely dispersed. It is interesting to ask precisely how delicately the rate of expansion has been "fine-tuned" to fall on this narrow dividing line between two catastrophes. If at time I S (by which time the pattern of expansion was already firmly established) the expansion rate had differed from its actual value by more than 10^{18} [1 followed by 18 zeros], it would have been sufficient to throw the delicate balance out. The explosive vigour of the Universe is thus matched with almost unbelievable accuracy to its gravitating power. The big bang was not, evidently, any old bang, but an explosion of exquisitely arranged magnitude.[11]

Davies acknowledged that the recent discoveries in astronomy strongly support the conclusion that there *must* be a supernatural Designer who created the Universe in the remarkably fine-tuned manner that allows the Earth and humanity to exist.

There is for me powerful evidence that there is something going on behind it all. . . . It seems as though somebody has *fine-tuned* nature's numbers to make the Universe. . . . The impression of design is overwhelming.[12]

In his book, *God and the New Physics*, Dr. Davis confirmed the overwhelming evidence of God's design of our world:

It is hard to resist the impression that the present structure of the Universe, apparently so sensitive to minor alterations in the numbers, has been rather carefully thought out. . . . The seemingly miraculous concurrence of numerical values that nature has assigned to her fundamental constants must remain the most compelling evidence for an element of cosmic design.[13]

The Density of Space Confirms Supernatural Creation

A spectacular new discovery by astronomers provides

compelling evidence in support of the supernatural intelligent design of the creation of the Universe. American researchers have used the Wilkinson Microwave Anisotropy Probe (WMAP) on a NASA satellite to measure the background radiation that remains from the initial moment of Creation. An article in the summer of 2003 by creationist astronomer Dr. Hugh Ross in *Connections* magazine reports the results of NASA's latest measurement and mapping of the background microwave radiation that is found throughout deep space. Dr. Ross wrote:

> The universe is comprised of 4 percent ordinary matter (protons, neutrons, and electrons that strongly interact with photons or light), 23 percent exotic matter (matter such as neutrinos that weakly interact with photons), and 73 percent space energy density (a self-stretching property of the space fabric of the universe).[14]

Dr. Ross summarized the theological significance of WMAP's discovery:

> The most spectacular evidence for supernatural design of the cosmos resides in its density characteristics. For physical life to be possible—anywhere, anytime—the mass density of the universe can differ by no more than one part in 10^{60}, and the space energy density by no more than one part in 10^{120}.[15]

This discovery confirms that our Universe was created by a supernatural intelligent Being in an incredibly precise design to allow life to exist.

The Distance of the Earth from the Sun
Allows Life to Exist

The Earth is 93 million miles distant from the Sun. This distance is precisely what is needed to allow biological life to exist on Earth. Life would be virtually impossible on any of the other planets in our solar system. Mercury and Venus are too close to the Sun and have surface temperatures that are far too high to allow life. Mars, Saturn, Jupiter, and the rest of the planets are too far from the Sun to receive the vital heat and energy to facilitate life. Earth is also the only planet in our solar system that has surface water in liquid form, an essential requirement for all life. *(See picture section, figure 11.)*

Earth's Circular Orbit

Every one of the other planets in our solar system circles the Sun in an elliptical orbit, not in the virtually perfect circular orbit of 93 million miles that the Earth does, our solar system's sole exception. If the Earth's orbit were elliptical, as are all of the other planets' orbits, such as Mars and Venus, then we would freeze for part of the year, as the Earth would move much further away from the Sun than it does now. Similarly, an elliptical orbit would cause a huge rise in temperature when that elliptical orbit would bring the Earth far too close to the Sun for the other part of the year. Our precise circular orbit at 93 million miles from the Sun provides a perfectly balanced temperature throughout the entire year.

A Supernova Explosion

Extremely rarely, an older star will gravitationally collapse upon its core in a stellar implosion in which the core of the star shrinks thousands of times within one second. A star much larger than our Sun (864,000 miles in diameter) will collapse to a diameter of only ten miles in a fraction of a second. The density of such a collapsed star would exceed hundreds of millions of tons per tablespoon of matter. How is this possible?

We need to remember that the incredibly small atoms that everything within our Universe is comprised of -- from the stars to your own body -- are composed of a nucleus at the center surrounded by electrons revolving at an almost inconceivable speed of 600 miles per second (2,160,000 miles per hour). However, the amount of empty space within the sphere of these astonishingly small atoms is enormous compared to the tiny nucleus at their center, and the even smaller electrons that circle them at such staggering velocities. For example, the simple hydrogen atom, which makes up the vast majority of the matter in the Universe, is composed of a nucleus with a single revolving electron. To illustrate how empty the atom actually is, imagine the nucleus of a hydrogen atom enlarged to the size of a tennis ball; the path of the single electron circulating around it would be at a circumference of more than four miles. In other words, the atom is mostly empty. (The atom is effectively 99.99999999 . . . empty.) This incredible gravitational collapse of the atoms in a collapsing star results in a staggering supernova explosion that radiates enormous amounts of heavy elements from the outer layers of the collapsed star far into the surrounding galaxy.

A supernova explosion is the sole method by which these heavy elements, such as iron, lead, and uranium, are produced in our galaxy. All that is solid in our world—the planets, the rocks and trees, as well as humanity—depend on the existence of these heavy elements sent through our galazy from these very rare stellar explosions. If there were no supernovas, then there would be no planets and no life organisms. Yet, if there were many more supernovas than is the case, there would be no life at all because the excess radiation would kill everything. *(See picture section, figure 21.)*

How rare are these essential supernova explosions? An employee of the Las Campanas Observatory in Chile was observing the night sky on the evening of February 23, 1987, and was startled to see a very bright star that he had never noticed before. Up until that moment the star was quite dim, but now it had become extremely bright. This significant increase in light was the result of an enormous supernova explosion deep in space. This was the first supernova explosion in our galaxy observed since the development of the telescope by the early astronomer Galileo more than three centuries ago.

Everywhere we look in the heavens or on Earth we discover evidence of the intelligent design of the Universe in a precise manner to allow not only the Earth to exist but to allow humanity to live on its surface. In the next chapter we will examine the evidence that scientists have recently discovered that provides evidence that God created the Universe with man at its center as part of His divine purpose.

Notes

1. George Politzer, *Principes Fondamentaux de Philosophie*, Editions Sociales, Paris, 1954, p. 84.
2. Arthur S. Eddington, as reported in S. Jaki, *Cosmos and Creator,* Chicago: Regnery Gateway, 1980.
3. Arthur Eddington, Internet site: http://www.windowview.org/science/heerenl.html
4. Albert Einstein Internet site: http://rescomp.stanford.edu/~cheshire/EinsteinQuotes.html
5. Isaac Newton, *Second Letter to Bentley.*
6. Stephen Hawking, *A Brief History of Time–From the Big Bang to Black Holes* (New York: Bantam Books, 1988), p. 122–123.
7. Lawrence J. Henderson, *The Fitness of the Environment: An Inquiry into the Biological Significance of the Properties of Matter,* [1913], Beacon Press: Boston, 1958, reprint, p.278.
8. F. Heeren, 1995. *Show Me God.* Wheeling, IL, Searchlight Publications, p. 200.
9. Hugh Ross, *The Creator and the Cosmos*, Navpress, 1995, p. 76.
10. Sir Fred Hoyle, quoted by W.R. Bird, *The Origin of Species Revisited*, Nashville: Thomas Nelson, 1991 p.462.
11. W. R. Bird, *The Origin of Species Revisited*, Nashville: Thomas Nelson. 1991, pp. 405-406.
12. Paul Davies, *The Cosmic Blueprint: New Discoveries in Nature's Creative Ability to Order the Universe* (New York: Simon and Schuster, 1988), p. 203.

13. Paul Davies, *God and the New Physics*, New York: Simon & Schuster, 1983, p 189.
14. Hugh Ross, "WMAP Offers Spectacular Proofs of Creation Event," *Connections*, second quarter, 2003.
15. Lawrence M. Krauss, "The End of the Age Problem and the Case for a Cosmological Constant Revisited," *Astrophysical Journal* 501 (1998), 461, 465.

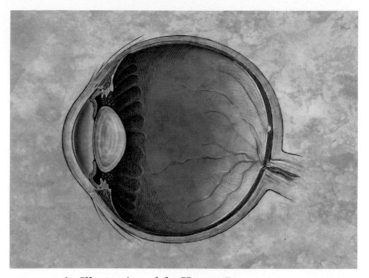

FIGURE 1. *An Illustration of the Human Eye.*

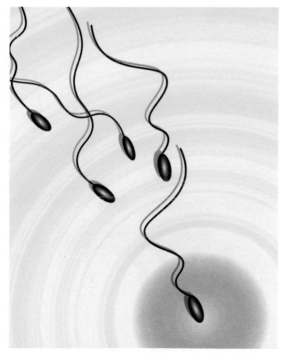

FIGURE 2.
*An Illustration of
the Sperm and Ova
at Fertilization.*

FIGURE 3.
*The Cuckoo Bird
(Great Roadrunner).*

FIGURE 4.
The Honey Bee.

FIGURE 5. *The Monarch Butterfly.*

FIGURE 6. *The Dolphin.*

FIGURE 7. *The Hummingbird.*

FIGURE 8. *The Canada Goose.*

FIGURE 9.
*An Illustration of
the Atom.*

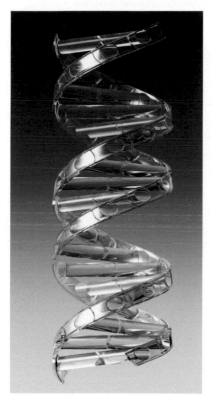

FIGURE 10.
*An Illustration of
the DNA Double Helix.*

FIGURE 11. *The Sun with a Huge Solar Flare.*

FIGURE 12.
*The Planets of
Our Solar System.*

FIGURE 13. *An Illustration of the Milky Way.*

FIGURE 14. *The Myth of the Ape Men.*
From the "Ascent of Man" Television Series.

FIGURE 15. *The Earth.*

Credit: NASA and STScI

FIGURE 16. *A View of Mars from the Hubble Telescope.*
http://hubblesite.org/newscenter/archive/2001/24/

FIGURE 17. *The Pencil Nebula—Remnant of the Huge Vela Supernova.*
http://hubblesite.org/newscenter/archive/2003/16/

Credit: NASA and STScI

FIGURE 18. *A Deep View of Space from the Hubble Telescope.*
http://hubblesite.org/newscenter/archive/1999/02/

FIGURE 19. *The Eagle Nebula.*
http://hubblesite.org/newscenter/archive/1995/44/

FIGURE 20. *The Hubble Telescope View of Abell 1689,*
a massive galaxy cluster.
http://hubblesite.org/newscenter/archive/2003/01/

Credit: NASA and STScI

FIGURE 21. *A Supernova Observed in 1987,*
the first supernova to be observed since A.D. *1604 in our galaxy.*
http://hubblesite.org/newscenter/archive/1999/04/

FIGURE 22.
*A Spiral Galaxy,
similar to our
Milky Way galaxy.*
*http://hubblesite.org/
newscenter/archive/
2002/03/*

Credit: NASA and STScI

Credit: NASA and STScI

FIGURE 23.
*Jupiter,
as photographed
by the Hubble
Telescope.*
*http://hubblesite.org/
newscenter/archive/
1991/13/*

FIGURE 24. *Saturn and its Rings.*
http://hubblesite.org/newscenter/archive/1998/18/

FIGURE 25. *Spiral Galaxy NGC 3370.*
http://hubblesite.org/newscenter/archive/2003/24/

4

Anthropic Principle: The Evidence of God's Fine-Tuning

And God saw every thing that he had made, and, behold, it was very good. And the evening and the morning were the sixth day (Genesis 1:31).

For thus saith the Lord that created the heavens; God himself that formed the Earth and made it; he hath established it, he created it not in vain, *he formed it to be inhabited*: I am the Lord; and there is none else (Isaiah 45:18, emphasis added).

The heaven, even the heavens, are the Lord's: but

the Earth hath he given to the children of men (Psalm 115:16).

The Scriptures continually assert that God purposely created the heavens and the Earth. In addition, the Bible affirms that God "formed it to be inhabited" (Isaiah 45: 18). For most of the last century, the majority of scientists rejected the concept of a supernatural Creator and the idea that all that we see in the Universe was created by a supernatural God for mankind. However, as this chapter will demonstrate, the last few decades have witnessed an extraordinary revolution in the thinking of many scientists, whose discoveries in astronomy, the nature of the atom, the genetic code in DNA, and the complexity of biological systems have made the concept of a purposeless, random, accidental Universe logically untenable. The accumulation of these numerous scientific discoveries in many fields has motivated a great number of scientists to reject their previous naturalistic, atheistic concepts in favor of the idea that the evidence supports the view that this Universe was somehow shaped to produce the conditions that favor life and especially humanity. This theory is called the "anthropic principle," a revolutionary change in the thinking of leading scientists regarding their analysis about the nature and purpose of the Universe.

The Anthropic Principle

The anthropic principle states that overwhelming scientific evidence demonstrates that the precise design and finely balanced fundamental forces governing our

Universe argue persuasively that our Universe was either designed by a supernatural intelligence, namely God, or that there are an infinity of Universes that don't support life and we just happen to exist in the only one that does.

The claim by those who admit that our Universe was "fine-tuned" to "one in a trillion" to allow life, but who suggest that we should ignore this evidence, is laughable. If someone was to suggest in any other area of life that we should accept the theoretical (and inevitably unprovable) existence of an infinity of imaginary Universes of which we are the only one that accidentally allows human life, they would be rejected with derision. Their theory of an infinity of other (forever unprovable) Universes demonstrates their absolute determination to reject God, regardless of the evidence.

The anthropic principle strongly suggests that a supernatural, superintelligent Being must have created our Universe to produce humanity because the conditions that make our Universe and human life possible are the result of spectacular "fine-tuning" of more than one hundred scientifically vital values, such as the composition of our atmosphere, the distance to the Sun, the chemical composition of the atmosphere, the strength of gravity, magnetism, and many other scientific constants.

Every one of these fundamental values is so precisely balanced that it is impossible to believe that this fine-tuning has occurred as a result of random chance. The more logical conclusion is that these fine-tuned essential values, such as the force of gravity, magnetism, and the strong and weak nuclear force, are the result of a supernatural Being in control of these fundamental factors that govern the very nature of our Universe. As this chapter will demonstrate, it appears from the scientific evidence developed during the last few decades that even the smallest possible change in the Universe's basic values would have resulted in the total elimination of the possibility of atoms, galaxies, stars, Earth, and human life.

Early in the last century most scientists rejected the existence of God due to their belief that the existing scientific discoveries suggested that the Universe had always existed and therefore there was no need for a Creator. They believed that Charles Darwin had demonstrated that natural selection and billions of years could account for the evolution of all complex biological lifeforms, including man. In addition, most intellectuals dismissed the concept that our Earth was the focus of God's creation. In 1935, Professor Bertrand Russell, a famous philosopher and prominent atheist, expressed the attitude of most intellectuals of his generation when he wrote the following statement in his book *Religion and Science*:

> Before the Copernican revolution, it was natural to suppose that God's purposes were specifically concerned with the Earth, but now this has become an unplausible hypothesis.[1]

The seventeenth-century Polish astronomer Copernicus created a philosophical revolution because his research provided compelling evidence that the Earth was not the center of our solar system, as almost everyone had previously assumed. Copernicus proved that the Earth rotated around the Sun and, therefore, the Sun was the center of our solar system. At first, many resisted his discovery because they feared that this was a contradiction to the revelation in the Bible. However, the Bible never claimed that the Sun revolved around the Earth. Over time, though, many people came to reject the Bible's assertion that God created the Earth and Universe primarily for humanity because the man-centered claim of the Scriptures seemed to be contradicted by the discovery that the Earth wasn't the center of our solar system.

As this book will demonstrate, the recent scientific discoveries have produced compelling new evidence in favor of the conclusion that both the Universe and our Earth were purposely created for humanity by a super intelligent Creator that exists outside of our Universe.

Since the 1950s, scientists have increased their understanding of the Universe through massive additions to our scientific knowledge in a variety of fields, including astrophysics, quantum physics, and microbiological genetic research. The sum total of our scientific knowledge is now doubling every twenty-four months—a staggering increase in information unprecedented in human history. It is interesting to note that the prophet Daniel prophesied 26 centuries ago that in the last days "knowledge shall increase." (Daniel 12:4)

The Birth of the Anthropic Principle

In 1973, a very important scientific conference was held in Poland that celebrated the five hundredth year since the birthday of Nicolaus Copernicus, the first and greatest astronomer of his age. A respected astrophysicist from Cambridge University, Dr. Brandon Carter, delivered a paper called "Large Number Coincidences and the Anthropic Principle in Cosmology." Dr. Carter coined the phrase "anthropic principle," derived from the Greek word *anthropos*, which means "man." Dr. Carter proposed an extraordinary theory: that the only rational way to explain the fact that the Universe existed as it does, with an incredibly precise balance between all of the multitude of forces including gravity, electromagnetism, and the strong nuclear force that made our Universe possible, can only be explained if they were fine-tuned in such a precise manner to allow human life to exist on Earth.

Recent discoveries in the field of astronomy, for example, prove that human life could not survive if the characteristics of our solar system were even slightly different. An astronomer, Dr. Jastrow, declared that even an extremely small increase in the strength of the nuclear forces that hold together all atoms would result in a Universe of stars composed primarily of helium instead of hydrogen. In a Universe with slightly increased nuclear forces, the helium stars would have burned up much more quickly than our hydrogen stars. However, if the nuclear forces were even slightly weaker, carbon atoms would not have formed, and without carbon atoms, no life could possibly exist in our Universe.

The same anthropic principle can be seen in the other scientific variables such as the force of gravity. Life would be impossible if the force of gravity were either much greater or much weaker. The electrical communication between every one of the sixty trillion cells in our body depends on the Earth's magnetic field. A reduction of the strength of the magnetic field beyond a certain level would make life impossible. No life could exist if our Earth were either too close or too far from the Sun, which provides the necessities of life through a complete spectrum of electromagnetic radiation, including visible light. The twenty-four hour rotation of our planet also facilitates life. If the planet did not rotate every twenty-four hours, one half of the globe would be desolate of vegetation under the constant glare of the Sun and the other half would freeze in perpetual darkness. In sum total, the scientists have concluded that there are many dozens of these scientific factors that are set within precise parameters to facilitate our life on this planet.

Professor Robert Jastrow, although he is an agnostic, admits that

the Universe was constructed within very narrow limits, in such a way that man could dwell in it. This result is called the anthropic principle. It is the most theistic result ever to come out of science, in my view.[2]

In other words, this evidence in support of the anthropic principle strongly supports the conclusion that our Universe and Earth were designed to provide a home for humanity by an intelligent and supernaturally powerful Creator. The evidence of intelligent design strongly suggests the existence of an intelligent Designer, namely God.

A later chapter in this book on the collapse of evolution will demonstrate that recent discoveries of science provide overwhelming evidence that the view of the atheists that our Universe and life could ever have accidentally developed by random chance over billions of years is scientifically impossible. In summary, these new scientific discoveries will demolish the evolutionary theory of the formation of life through random mutation and natural selection. These discoveries provide incontrovertible evidence that an intelligent Creator purposely designed and created both the Universe and human life on this planet.

The Universe Appears to be Designed by God

The Canadian religious philosopher John Leslie wrote about the timid religious leaders who were afraid to use the argument for intelligent design because they wrongly believed that modern scientific discoveries had disproved the Bible's account of Creation. Professor Leslie wrote:

> Contemporary religious thinkers often approach the Argument from Design with a grim determination that their churches shall not again be made to look foolish. Recalling what happened when churchmen opposed first Galileo and then Darwin, they insist that religion must be based not on science but on faith. Philosophy, they announce, has demonstrated that Design Arguments lack all force. I hope to have shown that philosophy has demonstrated no such thing. Our Universe, which these religious thinkers believe to be created by God, does look, greatly though

this may dismay them, very much as if created by God.[3]

Michael J. Denton, a prominent molecular biologist, wrote a book entitled *Evolution: A Theory in Crisis*, in which he concluded that overwhelming evidence has now been found demonstrating a purposeful design in the nature of our Universe that allows the galaxies, the Earth, and humanity itself to exist. Denton argued that the anthropic principle was philosophically sound and reasonable. Speaking of the 18th-century Christian theologian Paley's writings (Paley, *Natural Theology*) about the evidence for God's existence, Professor Denton, wrote:

> Paley was not only right in asserting the existence of an analogy between life and machines, but was also remarkably prophetic in guessing that the technological ingenuity realized in living systems is vastly in excess of anything yet accomplished by man. . . . The almost irresistible force of the analogy has completely undermined the complacent assumption, prevalent in biological circles over most of the past century, that the design hypothesis can be excluded on the grounds that the notion is fundamentally a metaphysical *a priori* concept and therefore scientifically unsound. On the contrary, the inference to design is a purely *a posteriori induction* based on a ruthlessly consistent application of the logic of analogy. The conclusion may have religious implications, but it does not depend on religious presuppositions.[4]

The philosopher Robert Augros and his colleague, the physicist Dr. George Stanciu, wrote that the cause and design of the physical Universe must come from something outside the Universe that bears an analogy to the similar relationship of our immaterial mind that controls the actions of our physical brain and body. They wrote:

> Matter does not need special instructions to manufacture snow flakes or sodium chloride. These forms are within its power. Not so with organic forms. Thus living forms transcend all other natural forms, not merely because of their unique activities . . . but also because the laws of physics and chemistry alone cannot produce them. What does produce them? What cause is responsible for the origin of the genetic code and directs it to produce animal and plant species? It cannot be matter because of itself matter has no inclination to these forms, any more than it has to the form Poseidon or to the form of a microchip or any other artifact. There must be a cause apart from matter that is able to shape and direct matter. Is there anything in our experience like this?

> Yes, there is: our own minds. The statue's form originates in the mind of the artist, who then subsequently shapes matter, in the appropriate way. The artist's mind is the ultimate cause of that form existing in matter, even if he or she invents a machine to manufacture the statues. For the same reasons there must be a mind that directs

and shapes matter into organic forms. Even if it does so by creating chemical mechanisms to carry out the task with autonomy, this artist will be the ultimate cause of those forms existing in matter. This artist is God, and nature is God's handiwork.[5]

The astronomer Dr. Paul Davis has written about the strong evidence that points to the fact that this Universe looks like it was designed by a superintelligent Designer with a very specific purpose involving humanity.

There is for me powerful evidence that there is something going on behind it all. . . . It seems as though somebody has fine-tuned nature's numbers to make the Universe. . . . The impression of design is overwhelming.[6]

Professor Davis also wrote,

The laws which enable the Universe to come into being spontaneously seem themselves to be the product of exceedingly ingenious design. If physics is the product of design, the Universe must have a purpose, and the evidence of modern physics suggests strongly to me that the purpose includes us.[7]

Sir Fred Hoyle, while a committed evolutionist, was honest enough to admit that scientific discoveries pointed to the fact that our Universe reflects intelligent purpose.

A common sense interpretation of the facts [concerning the energy levels in 12 Carbon and

16 Oxygen] suggests that a super intellect has monkeyed with physics, as well as with chemistry and biology, and that there are no blind forces worth speaking about in nature.[8]

In other words, the existence of carbon proves intelligent design.

Another science writer, John Horgan, wrote about Sir Fred Hoyle's acknowledgement of the fine-tuning of the Universe that allowed humanity to both exist and flourish on Earth. Horgan wrote:

> Purpose pervades Hoyle's Universe. He has long felt that natural selection alone could not account for the appearance and rapid evolution of life on the Earth. Some supernatural intelligence must be directing the evolution of life and indeed of the entire cosmos although to what end Hoyle does not know. The Universe is an obvious fix, he remarks. 'There are too many things that look accidental that are not.' Sensible scientists will dismiss such talk as preposterous. But every now and then, in their inevitable moments of doubt, they may wonder: Could Sir Fred be right?[9]

Astronomer Alan Sandage wrote:

> I find it quite improbable that such order came out of chaos. There has to be some organizing principle. God to me is a mystery but is the explanation for the miracle of existence, Why there is something instead of nothing?[10]

Biology professor John Maynard Smith wrote about

the remarkably precise nature of the physical Universe that supported galaxies, stars, planets, and human life.

> It turns out that the physical constants have just the values required to ensure that the Universe contains stars with planets capable of supporting intelligent life. . . . The simplest interpretation is that the Universe was designed by a creator who intended that intelligent life should evolve. This interpretation lies outside science.[11]

In their book, *Cosmic Coincidences: Dark Matter, Mankind, and Anthropic Cosmology*, cosmologist John Gribbin and astronomer Sir Martin Rees wrote about the infinite complexity and interconnectedness of every one of the fundamental forces that are so arranged to provide what is essential to the existence of our Universe and to human life itself.

> The conditions in our Universe really do seem to be uniquely suitable for life forms like ourselves, and perhaps even for any form of organic complexity.[12]

The Only Two Logical Alternatives: A God-Created Universe or an Infinity of Accidental Universes

Professor Paul C. W. Davies, the author of *God and the New Physics,* wrote that powerful evidence from new scientific discoveries confirmed that the remarkable nature of the known Universe provided only two rationally possible conclusions: 1) a divinely created Universe, or

2) an accidental and randomly formed Universe within an infinite number of other randomly formed Universes that did not contain the conditions required for life. The atheistic scientists acknowledge that it is scientifically impossible to ever find evidence for the existence of a single additional Universe, let alone an infinity of other hypothetical Universes. This assertion of a belief in an infinity of untold trillions of other random Universes takes more faith than to believe in God as Creator. It reveals the pathetic intellectual desperation of those atheists who desire to escape the overwhelming scientific evidence that points to a Creator of our Universe.

Davies wrote:

Alternatively the numerical coincidences could be regarded as evidence of design. The delicate fine-tuning in the values of the constants, necessary so that the various branches of physics can dovetail so felicitously, might be attributed to God. It is hard to resist the impression that the present structure of the Universe, apparently so sensitive to minor alterations in the numbers, has been rather carefully thought out. Such a conclusion can of course, only be subjective. In the end it boils down to a question of belief. Is it easier to believe in a cosmic designer than the multiplicity of Universes necessary for the weak anthropic principle to work? It is hard to see how either hypothesis could ever be tested in the strict scientific sense. As remarked in the previous chapter, if we cannot visit the other Universes or experience them directly, their possible existence must remain just as much a matter of faith as belief in God. Perhaps future developments in science will lead to more direct evidence for other Universes, but until then, the seemingly miraculous concurrence of numerical values that nature has assigned to her fundamental constants must remain the most compelling evidence for an element of cosmic design.[13]

Dr. Roger Penrose wrote in his book, *The Emperor's New Mind,* about his final conclusion regarding the precise accuracy of the nature of Creation.

This now tells us how precise the Creator's aim must have been, namely to an accuracy of one part in 10^{123}. This is an extraordinary figure. One could not possibly even write the number down in full in the ordinary denary notation: it would be 1 followed by 10^{123}; 10×123 zeros.[14]

Facts Pointing to Intelligent Design of the Universe

The strong nuclear force

Astronomer Sir Martin Rees noted in his book *Just Six Numbers: The Deep Forces That Shape the Universe* that the strength of the fundamental strong nuclear force, which expresses the strength of the electrical force that holds atoms together, was precisely balanced and calibrated to the force of gravity to allow the existence of the Universe.

The cosmos is so vast because there is one crucially important huge number N in nature, equal to 1,000,000,000,000,000,000,000,000,000,000,000,000,000. This number measures the strength of the electrical forces that hold atoms together, divided by the force of gravity between them. If N had a few less zeros, only a short-lived miniature Universe could exist: no creatures could grow larger than insects, and there would be no time for biological evolution.[15]

The weak nuclear force

Sir Martin Rees also commented on another fundamental force in the Universe, the weak nuclear force, that was also precisely calibrated to allow our Universe to exist and humanity to flourish. If the nuclear weak force were even slightly stronger then the expansion force at the moment of Creation it would have burned up all of the hydrogen atoms in the Universe to leave only helium—a result that would have prevented our present Universe and life from ever existing. Rees wrote:

> Another number, E [the Weak Nuclear Force], whose value is 0.007, defines how firmly atomic nuclei bind together and how all the atoms on Earth were made. Its value reflects the power from the Sun and, more sensitively, how stars transmute hydrogen into all the atoms of the periodic table. Carbon and oxygen are common, whereas gold and uranium are rare, because of what happens in the stars. If E were 0.006 or 0.008, we could not exist.[16]

The gravitation force and electromagnetic force

The extraordinary precise balance between another two fundamental forces, the gravitation force and the electromagnetic force, allows stars like our Sun to exist and radiate energy. The gravitational force holds the star together while the electromagnetic force energizes the star to radiate its energy. The physicist Brandon Carter determined that if the gravitation force were even slightly stronger or weaker, then our Sun would be a red dwarf star or a blue giant, neither of which could provide the energy to sustain life on Earth. Professor Carter calculated that even a tiny adjustment in gravitation force by one part in 10^{40} would eliminate the possibility of life on Earth.[17]

There is an incredible balance and interplay between the fundamental universal forces that govern the nature of atoms, stars, and galaxies. The science writer John Leslie wrote in *Universes* about the remarkably delicately balanced ratios between these forces.

> Important, too, is that force strengths and particle masses are distributed across enormous ranges. The nuclear strong force is (roughly) a hundred times stronger than electromagnetism, which is in turn ten thousand times stronger than the nuclear weak force, which is itself some ten thousand billion billion billion times stronger than gravity. So we can well be impressed by any apparent need for a force to be 'just right' even to within a factor of ten, let alone to within one part in a hundred or in 10^{100}—especially when

nobody is sure why the strongest force tugs any more powerfully than the weakest.[18]

The amount of matter in the Universe

Professor Rees wrote about the significance of the amount of matter existing in the Universe:

> The cosmic number Ω (omega) measures the amount of material in our Universe—galaxies, diffuse gas, and 'dark matter'. Ω tells us the relative importance of gravity and expansion energy in the Universe. If this ratio were too high relative to a particular 'critical' value, the Universe would have collapsed long ago; had it been too low, no galaxies or stars would have formed. The initial expansion speed seems to have been finely tuned.[19]

Rees wrote about the astonishing qualities of the Universe that together allowed our present human inhabited Universe to exist.

> These six numbers constitute a 'recipe' for a Universe. Moreover, the outcome is sensitive to their values: if any one of them were to be `untuned', there would be no stars and no life.[20]

The astrophysicist Dr. Stephen Hawking, author of the bestselling *A Brief History of Time*, is certainly the most famous scientist of our generation. While rejecting the existence of God, Hawking does acknowledge that there is remarkable evidence of the fine-tuning of the key constants controlling the nature of the Universe.

Hawking wrote, "In fact, if one considers the possible constants and laws that could have emerged, the odds against a Universe that produced life like ours are immense."[21]

The elements hydrogen and oxygen are essential

The biologist Dr. Lawrence J. Henderson wrote about the remarkable appearance in our Universe of the absolutely essential elements necessary to the existence of our Universe and human life—hydrogen and oxygen—and the incredible odds against these particular elements being formed by random chance rather than through intelligent design:

> There is, in truth, not one chance in countless millions of millions that the many unique properties of carbon, hydrogen, and oxygen, and especially of their stable compounds water and carbonic acid, which chiefly make up the atmosphere of a new planet, should simultaneously occur in the three elements otherwise than through the operation of a natural law which somehow connects them together. There is no greater probability that these unique properties should be without due cause uniquely favorable to the organic mechanism. These are no mere accidents; an explanation is to seek. It must be admitted, however, that no explanation is at hand.[22]

Of course, to anyone who considers this situation objectively, an obvious explanation comes to mind: "In the beginning God created the heavens and the Earth." Oxygen is absolutely essential to life. It is one of the most reactive elements in that it will quickly combine chemically with other elements. It is the most abundant element on our planet, making up almost 46 percent of the Earth's crust, as it is found combined with other elements in rock. The rest of the oxygen is found combined with hydrogen in water and making up 21 percent of the atmosphere. (Nitrogen forms virtually all of the rest of the Earth's atmosphere.)

The theoretical physicist Stephen Hawking acknowledged that the fact that the proton in the atom is precisely 1,836 times heavier than the electron is essential to the formation of molecules that are the building blocks of all life. The precise ratio between the proton and the electron is a fundamental number governing our Universe. Hawking stated, "The remarkable fact is that the values of these numbers seem to have been very finely adjusted to make possible the development of life."[23]

The curious nature of water

The astronomer John D. Barrow has written about the significance of the anthropic principle in his book *The Anthropic Cosmological Principle*. He noted that water, one of the most vital elements in the existence for all life, is an incredibly unusual and unlikely element to have formed in our Universe unless it were purposely designed by God. Professor Barrow wrote:

> Water is actually one of the strangest substances known to science. This may seem a rather odd thing to say about a substance as familiar but it is surely true. Its specific heat, its surface tension, and most of its other physical properties have

values anomalously higher or lower than those of any other known material. The fact that its solid phase is less dense than its liquid phase (ice floats) is virtually a unique property. The fact that ice floats allows aquatic life to exist in cold temperature zones.

These aspects or the chemical and physical structure of water have been noted before, for instance by the authors of the *Bridgewater Treatises* in the 1830s and by Henderson in 1913, who also pointed out that these strange properties make water a uniquely useful liquid and the basis for living things.[24]

If water as a solid (ice) were not less dense than as a liquid, ice would not float. Without this unique quality marine life would die as water would freeze from the bottom and kill all aquatic creatures in cold climates. Water is the most abundant substance on the Earth's surface and is essential for all life. The proteins and nucleic acids in DNA that govern all life could not exist without the unique qualities of water.

The size of the Sun and Earth

The size of the Earth is vital for life to exist. A much smaller planet would not have the gravitational pull to retain the water and atmosphere essential to life. A smaller Earth would produce a much thinner atmosphere that would diminish our protection from the thousands of meteors that daily assault our planet. The thinned atmosphere would produce less protection from the Sun, causing the temperature to rise till life could not flourish. A much larger planet would have a much more powerful gravitational field that would greatly increase the weight of every creature, making life almost impossible. If planet Earth were twice as large, the effect of increased gravity would make every organism on it's surface weigh eight times what it weighs today. This increased weight would destroy many forms of animal and human life. In addition, if the magnetic forces within our planet were significantly stronger or weaker, life could not exist. *(See picture section, figure 15.)*

The distance of the Earth from the Sun

If our Earth were located much farther away from our Sun, we would experience temperatures such as the minus 70°F measured on the planet Mars, and we would freeze. If the Earth were much closer to the Sun, then we would have temperatures like the extremely hot surface of Mercury or the 860-degree temperature on Venus, and we would burn up.

Our Earth's circular orbit is very unusual and it makes life possible on our home planet. All of the other planets in our solar system have elliptical orbits that take them much further away from the Sun for part of their orbit and much closer to the Sun for the other part of their orbit. If our Earth followed an elliptical orbit as the other planets in our solar system do, life would be impossible because it would be too cold for part of the year and far to hot the other part of the year. Our unique circular orbit keeps us 93 million miles from the Sun, precisely the right distance to maintain the temperature range conducive to life.

The 23-degree inclination of the Earth

Our Earth is tilted from an upright position at a 23-degree inclination. This tilt provides for the seasonal variation that allows such a wide variety of crops to feed life. This 23-degree tilt prevents the North and South Poles from becoming too cold and moderates the high temperatures at the Equator. It has been estimated that almost half of the Earth's surface would become uninhabitable without the tilt of the Earth. Without the tilt, less than half of the present land used for cultivation of crops would grow vegetables.

The rotation speed of the Earth

Our Earth rotates at 1,002 miles per hour, which allows our planet to rotate completely once every twenty-four hours. If our planet did not rotate, then one half of the stationary Earth facing the Sun would become so hot that no vegetation or any other life could possibly survive. The side of the non-rotating planet facing away from the Sun would be so cold that life could not exist.

Why does everything in our Universe, from galaxies to our solar system, orbit at precisely the correct velocity to perfectly counterbalance the force of gravity? If the velocity of our solar system's planets or our massive, revolving Milky Way galaxy, with its 300+ billion stars, was slightly less than the force of gravity, then the various components would rapidly be drawn by gravity toward the center of the system. This would result in each system's collapse and destruction. If the velocity of each orbiting system were slightly greater than gravity, the components would fly apart into space, thus destroying each system. When we consider the remarkable balance between velocity and gravity that exists in billions of systems throughout the Universe, we are forced to admit that there is no reason why this elaborately tuned and balanced system should exist unless a divine Creator supernaturally designed it. A precise controlling power is thus demonstrated to be holding together every astronomical system throughout the known Universe.

The balance of gases in Earth's atmosphere

The atmosphere of the Earth is composed of precisely the right gases necessary for life to flourish. In addition, these gases exist in precisely the correct ratio to facilitate the complex biological processes that are essential for the enormously complex demands of plant and animal life as well as for humans. The atmosphere is composed of: 78 percent nitrogen, 21 percent oxygen, a small amount of other gases, and water. Sigmund Brouwer wrote, in his book *The Unrandom Universe*, that the odds against this essential atmosphere together with the water cycle forming on Earth by random chance alone are approximately one chance in a hundred trillion trillion.[25]

The existence of carbon

All life systems on Earth are based on the existence of the element known as carbon. However, scientists discovered that it is extremely unlikely that carbon could have come into existence by random chance in the beginning of the Universe. Professor Steven Weinberg wrote about the absolute necessity of carbon for life to exist at all.

Life as we know it would be impossible if any one of several physical quantities had slightly different values. The best known of these quantities is the energy of one of the excited states of the carbon 12 nucleus. There is an essential step in the chain of nuclear reactions that build up heavy elements in stars.[26]

In the first fraction of a second following Creation, the Universe consisted only of hydrogen and helium. However, the collision of a helium nucleus with another helium nucleus produced an extremely short-lived and very unstable new element called beryllium. Another helium nucleus then collided with the beryllium nucleus, producing a new element: carbon. All of this took place in the first second of God's Creation. A Harvard University astronomer, Robert Kirshner, wrote,

> A delicate match between the energies of helium, the unstable beryllium and the resulting carbon allows the last to be created. Without this process, we would not be here.[27]

The incredibly unlikely creation of carbon also resulted in the formation of all of the other heavy elements in the Universe that are essential for life to exist, including nitrogen and oxygen. The astrophysicist Sir Fred Hoyle admitted that, when he considered how totally unlikely it was that the element carbon could have been formed by accident, his atheism was shaken to the core. He wrote,

> A common sense interpretation of the facts suggests that a super intellect has monkeyed with

physics, as well as with chemistry and biology, and that there are no blind forces worth speaking about in nature. The numbers one calculates from the facts seem to me so overwhelming as to put this conclusion almost beyond question.[28]

Significantly, the most respected physicist in the world, Stephen Hawking, summarized the implications of his remarkable discoveries about the Universe's first moments.

The odds against a Universe like ours emerging out of something like the big bang are enormous. . . . I think clearly there are religious implications whenever you start to discuss the origins of the Universe. There must be religious overtones. But I think most scientists prefer to shy away from the religious side of it.[29]

However, the accumulated evidence supporting the intelligent design of the Universe and the anthropic principle is convincing many leading scientists to abandon atheistic, materialistic worldview and accept the fact that our Universe is the purposeful creation of God. Dr. Chandra Wickramasinghe, one of the most eminent scientists in Britain, has stated that the anthropic principle strongly supports the theory of God's special creation, as opposed to evolution. When he was asked if his scientific research proved that Charles Darwin's theory of evolution was fatally flawed, he agreed. When asked how he would evaluate the scientific arguments of the Creationists, who suggest that only God could have created the Universe and life itself, Professor

Wickramasinghe responded, "You mean the arguments that are justifications of their position? I think they have a very good case by and large."[30]

Scientists' Support for Intelligent Design

Dr. Paul Davies wrote about his personal beliefs and his estimate of the views about Creation of other physicists in his fascinating 1983 article entitled "The Christian Perspective of a Scientist" in the evolution supporting magazine *New Scientist*. Dr. Davies wrote,

> The temptation to believe that the Universe is the product of some sort of design, a manifestation of subtle aesthetic and mathematical judgment, is overwhelming. The belief that there is 'something behind it all' is one that I personally share with, I suspect, a majority of physicists.[31]

Professor Robert Jastrow summarized the anthropic principle and the argument for intelligent design of the Universe when he stated that

> the smallest change in any of the circumstances of the natural world, such as the relative strengths of the forces of nature, or the properties of the elementary particles, would have led to a Universe in which there could be no life and no man. For example, if nuclear forces were decreased by a few percent, the particles of the Universe would not have come together in nuclear reactions to make the ingredients, such as carbon atoms, of which life must be constructed.[32]

Professor Jastrow also noted that the same argument can be made about the strength of the electromagnetic force and the strength of the gravitational force. In other words, if the Universe was altered in the slightest way, no animal or human life could ever have formed on planet Earth.

A NASA astronomer and scientist, Professor John O'Keefe, has acknowledged the utter impossibility that the Universe would ever have developed in a manner that would have allowed humanity to exist by random chance. Dr. O'Keefe wrote,

> We are, by astronomical standards, a pampered, cosseted, cherished group of creatures. . . . If the Universe had not been made with the most exacting precision, we could never have come into existence. It is my view that these circumstances indicate the Universe was created for man to live in.[33]

Professor Arno Penzias, who won the Nobel prize for physics, acknowledged that astronomy reveals that our Universe was created "out of nothing" and is apparently designed by some supernatural being to allow humanity to exist and prosper. Dr. Penzias wrote,

> Astronomy leads us to a unique event, a Universe which was created out of nothing, one with the very delicate balance needed to provide exactly the conditions required to permit life, and one which has an underlying (one might say 'supernatural') plan.[34]

Professor Wernher von Braun was the leading

post-WWII German rocket scientist who developed the American NASA program that ultimately developed the *Saturn V* moon rocket. Professor von Braun wrote:

> I find it as difficult to understand a scientist who does not acknowledge the presence of a superior rationality behind the existence of the Universe as it is to comprehend a theologian who would deny the advances of science.[35]

The astronomer Professor Alan Sandage acknowledged the powerful evidence of design that scientists discovered in our Universe.

> I find it quite improbable that such order came out of chaos. There has to be some organizing principle. God to me is a mystery but is the explanation for the miracle of existence, why there is something instead of nothing.[36]

The most famous astronomer and theoretical physicist in our generation is Professor Stephen Hawking. He has introduced millions of readers to the wonders of the Universe through his tremendous book *A Brief History of Time*. Dr. Hawking carefully examined the compelling evidence that our Universe appears to have been designed. While refusing to acknowledge God, Professor Hawking stated:

> The laws of science, as we know them at present, contain many fundamental numbers, like the size of the electric charge of the electron and the ratio of the masses of the proton and the electron. . . . The remarkable fact is that the values of these

numbers seem to have been very finely adjusted to make possible the development of life.[37]

The ultimate conclusion of these scientists is that our Universe, solar system and, especially, our Earth was purposely constructed by a very powerful intelligence within very narrow scientific parameters to allow human life to flourish.

Notes

1. Bertrand Russell, *Religion and Science.*
2. Robert Jastrow, quoted in *The Intellectuals Speak out about God,* (Chicago: Regnery Gateway, 1984)
3. John Leslie, " Universes" (1989), Routledge: London, 1996, reprint, p. 22.
4. Michael J. Denton, *Evolution: A Theory in Crisis,* Burnett Books: London, 1985, p. 341.
5. Robert Augros and George Stanciu, *The New Biology: Discovering the Wisdom in Nature,* New Science Library, Shambhala: Boston, 1987, pp. 190–191.
6. Paul C. W. Davies. *The Cosmic Blueprint: New Discoveries in Nature's Creative Ability to Order the Universe.* New York: Simon and Schuster, 1988. p. 203.
7. Paul C. W. Davies, *Super force: The Search for a Grand Unified Theory of Nature,* [1984], Penguin: London, 1995, reprint, p. 243.
8. Fred Hoyle, *"The Universe: Past and Present Reflections,"* Annual Review of Astronomy and Astrophysics, Vol. 20, 1982, p.1-355, p. 16.
9. John Horgan, "The Return of the Maverick," *Scientific American*, Vol. 272, No. 324, March 1995, p. 24–25.
10. J. N. Willford, March 12, 1991. "Sizing up the Cosmos: An Astronomers Quest." *New York Times,* p. B9.
11. John Maynard Smith and Eors Szathmary, "On the likelihood of habitable worlds," *Nature*, Vol. 384, 14 November 1996, p. 107.

12. John Gribbin and Sir Martin Rees, *Cosmic Coincidences: Dark Matter, Mankind, and Anthropic Cosmology*, Bantam: New York, 1989, pp. 268–269.

13. Paul C. W. Davies, *God and the New Physics*, [1983], Penguin: London, 1990, reprint, p. 189.

14. Roger Penrose, *The Emperor's New Mind*, 1989.

15. Sir Martin Rees, *Just Six Numbers: The Deep Forces That Shape the Universe*, [1999], Phoenix: London, 2000, p. 2.

16. Sir Martin Rees, *Just Six Numbers: The Deep Forces That Shape the Universe*, [1999], Phoenix: London, 2000, p. 2.

17. Paul C. W. Davies, *God and the New Physics* (New York: Simon and Schuster, 1983), p. 188.

18. John Leslie, *Universes* (London: Routledge, 1996), p. 6.

19. Sir Martin Rees, *Just Six Numbers: The Deep Forces That Shape the Universe*, [1999], Phoenix: London, 2000, pp. 2–3.

20. Sir Martin Rees, *Just Six Numbers: The Deep Forces That Shape the Universe*, [1999], Phoenix: London, 2000, p. 4.

21. Stephen Hawking, http://www.evolutionisdead.com/quotes.php?QID=284&cr=74

22. Lawrence J. Henderson, *The Fitness of the Environment: An Inquiry into the Biological Significance of the Properties of Matter*, [1913], Beacon Press: Boston, 1958, reprint, p. 276.

23. Stephen Hawking, *A Brief History of Time – From the Big Bang to Black Holes* (New York: Bantam Books, 1988), p. 125

24. John D. Barrow and Frank J. Tipler, *The Anthropic Cosmological Principle*, [1986], Oxford University Press: Oxford UK, 1996, reprint, p. 524.

25. Sigmund Brouwer, *The Unrandom Universe*, Eugene: Harvest House Publishers, 2002, p. 64.

26. Steven Weinberg, "Life in the Universe," *Scientific American* (October 1994), p. 49

27. Robert Kirshner, "The Earth's Elements," *Scientific American* (October 1994), p. 61.

28. Fred Hoyle, "The Universe: Past and Present Reflections," *Annual Review of Astronomy and Astrophysics*, Vol. 20, 1982, p. 1–35, 16.

29. Stephen Hawking, quoted by John Boslough, *Masters of Time–Cosmology at the End of Innocence* (New York: Addison-Wesley Publishing Company, 1992), p. 55.

30. Chandra Wickramasinghe, The *Intellectuals Speak out about God,* (Chicago: Regnery Gateway, 1984), 36.

31. Paul Davies, *New Scientist*, June 1983, p. 638.

32. Robert Jastrow, *The Intellectuals Speak out about God*, (Chicago: Regnery Gateway, 1984), p. 21

33. John A. O'Keefe, cited by Robert Jastrow, *God and the Astronomers*, second edition (New York & London: W. W. Norton & Company, 1992), p. 118.

34. H. Margenau and R. A. Varghese, eds. *Cosmos, Bios, Theos: Scientists Reflect on Science, God, and the Origins of the Universe, Life, and Homo sapiens* (La Salle, Ill., Open Court Pub. Co., 1992). p. 83.

35. T. McIver, 1986, "Ancient Tales and Space-Age Myths of Creationist Evangelism", *The Skeptical Inquirer* 10:258–276.

36. J. N. Willford, "Sizing up the Cosmos: An Astronomers Quest", *New York Times*, March 12, 1991, p. B9.
37. Stephen Hawking, *A Brief History of Time—From the Big Bang to Black Holes* (New York: Bantam Books, 1988) p. 139.

5

DNA—
The Language of God

Thousands of years ago, God inspired Moses to record that vegetation was created first to support animal life and humanity.

> And God said, Behold, I have given you every herb bearing seed, which is upon the face of all the Earth, and every tree, in the which is the fruit of a tree yielding seed; to you it shall be for meat. And to every beast of the Earth, and to every fowl of the air, and to every thing that creepeth upon the Earth, wherein there is life, I have given every green herb for meat: and it was so (Genesis 1:29-30).

In Genesis, God declared that all of creation was placed under the dominion of man.

> And God said, Let us make man in our image, after our likeness: and let them have dominion over the fish of the sea, and over the fowl of the air, and over the cattle, and over all the Earth, and over every creeping thing that creepeth upon the Earth. So God created man in his own image, in the image of God created he him; male and female created he them (Genesis 1:26-27).

Atheists and agnostics often ask this question: If God truly exists and created this Universe, why does He not reveal Himself to us by sending us an intelligent message that no one else could possibly have sent? Most Christians would answer that God has already sent us two compelling messages: the written revelation of the supernaturally inspired Word of God, and the life and teaching of His Son Jesus Christ. However, many scientifically-minded atheists and agnostics are asking for something more. As a result of the most spectacular scientific discovery of the last century—the 1953 discovery of the double-helix structure of the genetic code (DNA) by Professors James Watson and Francis Crick—we are now in possession of a very clear information-filled message that is so staggering in its complexity that it cannot possibly have been produced without a supernatural intelligence. The discovery of the structure and function of DNA has revealed the "language of God" governing the creation of all life.

The Nature of DNA

The ability of biological organisms to reorganize and regenerate themselves has puzzled philosophers and scientists since ancient times. With the exception of mature red blood cells, the sixty trillion cells in our human body contain a nucleus that holds the forty-six vital threadlike chromosomes that contain our genetic instructions. DNA, the symbol for deoxyribonucleic acid, determines much of what plants, animals and humans are. DNA is a specialized molecule that stores enormous amounts of encoded hereditary information that controls the growth, repair, and reproduction of the body. DNA is composed of two long chains of specialized chemicals arranged into intricate pairs, forming a double helix that comprises the building blocks of the future organism. *(See picture section, figure 10.)*

For example, human DNA forms a double helix that is coiled together within the nucleus of every one of the sixty trillion cells that make up our body. Although incredibly small, if you were to stretch out the coiled DNA double helix it would be five to six feet long. Despite its length, the DNA structure is so thin that it would take over one trillion double helixes side by side to make a structure one inch thick.

Although human DNA appears to be the most complex, the DNA found in even the "simplest" form of bacteria is still enormously complex, as it contains at least three million units, with every single unit aligned in a very precise, meaningful sequence. To illustrate the staggering amount of detailed information encoded within the DNA molecule within our cells, consider the comments of two respected geneticists who have carefully examined the language of DNA. In an article entitled "The High Fidelity of DNA Duplication" published in 1988 in the *Scientific American* journal, Dr. Miroslav Radman and Dr. Robert Wagner wrote, "The set of genetic instructions for humans [in the DNA molecule] is roughly three billion letters long."[1] The latest research indicates that human DNA code contains five billion letters.

Forty years ago, when the world's population was only three billion people, Professor Ashley Montagu calculated the actual size of the vital DNA molecule that controls all human bodies. Dr. Ashley wrote:

> In fact, the chromosomes, the actual bearers of the hereditary particles, the genes, within the cells of this huge number [three billion] would occupy less space than half an aspirin tablet! Reflect upon that! All the hereditary materials—the heredity of the whole human race of all those now living could be contained within the space of half an aspirin.[2]

With today's population of approximately 6.3 billion, with one DNA molecule from each person, the genetic blueprint for every human on Earth could now fit into one aspirin tablet.

What are the odds that such an enormously complicated genetic code as DNA could have been formed by chance rather than by the purposeful creation by a Divine supernatural intelligence—God? Dr. George Howe, a botanist and biologist, has calculated the probability that the complex genetic information encoded within the DNA molecule could have been produced by chance over long periods of time:

> The chance that useful DNA molecules would develop without a Designer are approximately zero. Then let me conclude by asking which came first—the DNA (which is essential for the synthesis of proteins) or the protein enzyme (DNA-polymerase) without which DNA synthesis is nil? . . . there is virtually no chance that chemical 'letters' would spontoneously produce coherent DNA and protein 'words.'[3]

Dr. Michael Denton, a researcher in human molecular genetics, also wrote about the intricate protein synthesis apparatus that exists in everything that lives:

It is astonishing to think that this remarkable piece of machinery, which possesses the ultimate capacity to construct every living thing that ever existed on Earth, from a giant redwood to the human brain, can construct all of its own components in a matter of minutes and weigh less than 10^{-16} grams. It is of the order of several thousand million million times smaller than the smallest piece of functional machinery constructed by man.[4]

Sir Fred Hoyle, the famous astronomer and physicist, makes a very striking observation about the evolutionary theory of the accidental origin of life. In his book *The Intelligent Universe,* Hoyle wrote: "The chance that higher life forms might have emerged in this way (by coincidence) is comparable with the chance that a tornado sweeping through a junk-yard might assemble a Boeing 747 from the materials herein.[5]

Dr. Richard Lewontin, a prominent evolutionist

from Harvard University, confesses to the fact that it is unyielding prejudice and bias against the supernatural that is the true motive that causes many scientists to reject special creation out of hand.

> It is not that the methods and institutions of science somehow compel us to accept a material explanation of the phenomenal world, but, on the contrary, that we are forced by our *a priori* adherence to material causes to create an apparatus of investigation and a set of concepts that produce material explanations, no matter how counter-intuitive, no matter how mystifying to the uninitiated. Moreover, that materialism is absolute, so we cannot allow a Divine Foot in the door.[6]

In other words, it is not the evidence that forces scientists to insist on am evolutionary explanation for life, it is their strong prejudice against supernatural Creation.

American microbiologist Homer Jacobson wrote about the absolute impossibility that the multitude of materials and conditions could ever have come together to produce life without the intervention of supernatural design.

> The complete directions for the reproduction of plans, for energy and the extraction of parts from the current environment, for the growth sequence, and for the effect for mechanism translating instructions into growth—all had to be simultaneously present at that moment (when life began). This combination of events has

seemed an incredibly unlikely happenstance, and has often been ascribed to divine intervention.[7]

The Evidence of Intelligent Design Demonstrated in DNA

The ability of living organisms to reorganize, reproduce, and regenerate has astonished people since ancient times. Anyone who seriously contemplates the miracle of the growth of a huge tree from a tiny seed, the regeneration of the lost limbs of a salamander, or the growth of a baby in its mother's womb from a microscopic joined sperm and ova has wondered at the miracle of life.

One of the most essential features of genetic transmission is the need for a method of storing and transmitting complex genetic information. DNA is the genetic blueprint for life, holding unique instructions for building, repairing, and reproducing every living thing on Earth. All of the information needed for these vital biological functions is encoded in a double helix form. The DNA is composed of four subunits called nucleotides. These four nucleotide (except for red blood cells) are composed of a phosphate (P) with ribose sugar together with one of these four bases: guanine (G); cytosine (C); thymine (T); or adenine (A). The genetic message that conveys the ways organs and body structures form is encoded in the intricate sequence of the four chemical bases (G, C, T, and A) that are arranged as letters to convey precise instructions similar to the English language.

If the information encoded in this four-letter DNA code were printed out in letters, the genetic information for a "simple" bacteria would take several million letters, that, when printed out, would fill a book of at least a thousand pages. However, to record the genetic instructions encoded in human DNA we would need more than five billion letters that would require up to three thousand volumes to print out. This enormous amount of information would fill a library shelf over one hundred yards long. Yet it is intricately encoded in a tiny double helix curled up in a microscopic cell. This degree of microengineering is so far beyond the ability of humans that it fills the mind with wonder at the work of the Creator.

DNA encodes precise genetic information regarding biological functions in an analogous manner to the way in which the digital binary code of modern computer software uses 0s and 1s to convey complicated messages and mathematical information. However, instead of using 0s and 1s, DNA uses the almost infinite possible arrangements of the four bases (G, C, T, and A) as letters to store and transmit a staggering amount of precise genetic information governing how a plant, animal, or human will develop, repair itself, and reproduce. Some have compared the information-carrying capacity of DNA genetic instructions to a sophisticated computer software program such as General Motors uses to control its complete manufacturing, inventory, and accounting processes for all of its automobile manufacturing factories throughout the globe.

Scientists were astonished to discover that the entire genetic information required to build a human body, to repair it, and to reproduce it is contained in a DNA molecule that weighs less than several billionths of an ounce. In fact, it has been calculated that all of the one billion DNA molecules necessary to form every one of the approximately one billion separate aquatic, animal, and plant species that now exist or have ever existed on Earth could be compacted into an object the size of one grain of salt.[8]

Another key component in the transmission of genetic information is accomplished by an additional wonder of Creation: RNA (ribonucleic acid). This essential macromolecule is chemically similar to DNA but serves the function of a messenger that conveys the genetic message to make proteins that are the body's essential building blocks that form all of our biological systems.

The huge advances in genetic research in the last five decades have enabled scientists to begin to unlock some of the mysteries of the genetic code which governs the formation of every organ in your body, the color of your eyes, and whether you have black or blonde hair.

The new science called information theory allows scientists to mathematically analyze the information patterns of any written language such as English. Recently, researchers studied the information patterns encoded in the DNA of "simple" bacteria. To their surprise, the scientists discovered that similar complex mathematical information patterns exist in both human language as well as in DNA. The information patterns in a language such as English can be mathematically analyzed because the letters and words in a message form a purposeful pattern. Obviously, information conveyed in a written message in a language is purposeful, not random. If letters and words were thrown together by chance, they would not convey meaningful information. When we find letters forming words in patterns of sentences expressing meaningful information, we logically conclude that this information was created through purposeful design by an intelligent mind such as our own.

All living biological organisms are incredibly complex. When we examine the simplest bacteria, we discover an almost unbelievable complexity of miniaturized design that in comparison makes the technical specifications for a NASA space shuttle look relatively simple. Biologists now realize that the simplest cell is not simple at all. A single cell is an enormously complex structure that is actually far more complicated than any super computer. The smallest cell in your body is composed of over fifty billion atoms arranged into more than one hundred different proteins, together with a staggering amount of genetic information encoded in the DNA and RNA that govern the cell's activities, nutrition, repair, and replication. The inescapable problem for the theory of evolution is that every part of this complex cell needs to be present for the cell to function at all. You can't start with part of this cell because everything is interrelated and necessary for the cell to function as a whole.

Dr. Francis Crick, an atheist and co-discoverer of the structure of DNA, admitted that there is almost no possibility whatsoever that the very first life could have spontaneously generated from the inorganic chemicals that may have existed in the early Earth's atmosphere and surface water. As a result of his conclusion that life could never have spontaneously developed on Earth over billions of years, he was forced to develop an alternative theory to account for the existence of tremendously complex organisms found everywhere on Earth. Professor Crick wrote a book entitled *Life Itself* in which he explained his new theory that suggested that life was actually developed through evolution in some other galaxy and was then brought to Earth from outer space by means of alien starships or by solar winds. While such a theory is certainly imaginative, it is totally false. Dr. Crick acknowledges that his theory has no evidence whatsoever to support it, but he prefers it to admitting that only a supernatural God could rationally account for the beginning of life, the existence of DNA, and all of the millions of species found on Earth today.9 However, if you consider the situation for a moment, you will realize that if evolution cannot possibly explain the beginning of life on Earth, it is equally impossible that life evolved by random chance in any other galaxy or Universe. Crick has taken the impossible and made it even more fanciful.

Professor Richard Dawkins, a prominent Oxford evolutionist, acknowledged that the genetic code in DNA was a very sophisticated language that specified the precise nature of every single aspect of organisms. He admitted that the genetic information encoded in all DNA molecules was obviously as purposeful and as intelligent as any complex engineering manual written by a computer scientist. Dr. Dawkins wrote:

> After Watson and Crick, we know that genes themselves, within their minute internal structure, are long strings of pure digital information. What is more, they are truly digital, in the full and strong sense of computers and compact

disks, not in the weak sense of the nervous system. The genetic code is not a binary code as in computers, nor an eight-level code as in some telephone systems, but a quaternary code, [4. letter] with four symbols. The machine code of the genes is uncannily computerlike. Apart from differences in jargon, the pages of a molecular-biology journal might be interchanged with those of a computer engineering journal.[10]

When we consider the obvious evidence of super-natural design in the DNA genetic instructions that govern all life on Earth, the argument for a supernatural designer of life on Earth is compelling.

Proteins and Enzymes: Building Blocks of Life

Proteins and enzymes are absolutely essential as the building blocks of life. Enzymes are vital because they speed up the chemical reactions that are required for any kind of life process to exist. Enzymes are the biological catalysts for life. If these enzymes did not exist, the chemical reactions that are essential for life would not work or would operate so slowly that life would be impossible. Enzymes can speed up a chemical reaction rate by a factor of at least a thousand to a million times.[11]

Dr. Fred Holye and Dr. Chandra Wickramasinghe wrote in their book *Evolution from Space* about the total impossibility that these thousands of enzymes, the essential biological catalysts of life, could ever have been correctly arranged by chance even if billions of years were available.

The trouble is that there are about two thousand enzymes, and the chance of obtaining them all in a random trial is only one part in $(10^{20})^{2,000} = 10^{40,000}$, an outrageously small probability that could not be faced even if the whole Universe consisted of organic soup.[12]

The truth is that this calculation proves the total impossibility that life could ever have formed on Earth by chance regardless of how much time was available.

Dr. A. E. Wilder-Smith wrote about the tremendous complexity of biological cells:

> When one considers that the entire chemical information to construct a man, elephant, frog, or an orchid was compressed into two minuscule reproductive cells [sperm and egg nuclei], one can only be astounded. In addition to this, all the information is available on the genes to repair the body (not only to construct it) when it is injured. If one were to request an engineer to accomplish this feat of information miniaturization, one would be considered fit for the psychiatric clinic.[13]

The Complexity of the "Simple" Cell

When evolutionists wrote about their theory of the accidental development of life from lifeless inorganic matter, they often referred to the first random arrangement by chance of the twenty amino acids that formed the first complex proteins. Then they suggested these essential complex proteins finally formed into the so-called simple cells as if these first true living cells that make up all living creatures were composed of a simple jelly-like material called protoplasm (living substance). However, the scientific discoveries of the last few decades have totally destroyed any idea that the living cell (the essential building block of all living organisms) could ever be described as simple. The truth is that the simple cell is not so simple after all.

Scientists have recently discovered that the "simple" living cell is an enormously complex organization equivalent to a modern city. In fact, the simple cell is an incredibly well-engineered construction that defies the imagination in its intricate complex construction, its functions, its defense systems, its intricate transportation and waste disposal functions, its energy systems, and its intricate communication systems both within and without the cell.

The simple living cell contains an extraordinarily complex maze of intricate structures including tubes, miniature chemical factories, transportation systems, and communication systems that transmit complex genetic information involving millions of precise instructions between the master DNA and the messenger RNA within the cell that intertwine to complete their data transfer instantaneously. Biological research has determined that all of these complex and interconnected cellular functions are working in harmony twenty-four hours a day to allow the cell to complete its essential functions in whatever living organism it serves. Every single one of the dozens of cellular functions must operate in harmony with every other process to allow the microscopic living cell to function as required.

The living cells that are essential for all living organisms to exist contain thousands of even smaller proteins that are vital for all of the life functions of these cells. However, every one of those proteins is composed of as many as one thousand amino acid molecules arranged in complex sequences that will not function properly if the smallest error exists in their arrangement. The odds against these amino acids being arranged correctly by chance are astronomical. The living cells that make life possible could never function unless every single one of the essential proteins was present and functioned precisely to produce the necessary materials to support life. The living cells could never have operated to support life functions unless all of the amino acids were present in the precise sequence necessary to fully function.

The surface of the cell is astonishing in its precise ability to both control the entrance and exit of all the essential complex nutrients that must be absorbed, as well as toxins and waste that must be rejected. Although the cell's protective membrane is only one-third of a millionth of an inch thick, its remarkable sensory system is able to identify the nature of all of the molecules that surround it to determine which molecules should be absorbed for nutrition and which should be rejected as toxic.

When the cell detects a useful molecule, it reaches out for it utilizing a process whereby the cell expands toward the needed molecule, then surrounds and absorbs it.

The cell is as complicated as a modern city, with its

complex defenses, transportation systems, communication functions, energy supplies, waste disposal, libraries for storage of necessary data, and administrative control of the whole system.

The thousands of individual and absolutely essential proteins that make up every cell are themselves enormously complex and precisely arranged numbers of amino cells that could never have arranged themselves in the necessary order for life by chance alone.

The genetic code in the DNA within every cell communicates to the rest of the trillions of cells within our body through the RNA genetic transfer material found in every cell.

It is worth repeating the words of the scientist Professor Michael Denton, who declared:

It is astonishing to think that this remarkable piece of machinery, which possesses the ultimate capacity to construct every living thing that ever existed on Earth, from giant red wood trees to the human brain, can construct all its own components in a matter of minutes and weigh less than 10^{-16} grams. It is of the order of several thousand million million times smaller than the smallest piece of functional machinery ever constructed by man. (Until man invented nanotechnology.)[14]

Nanotechnology is the very recent invention of incredibly microscopic machines, but they are still billions of times larger than the DNA genetic machines that control all organisms.

Notes

1. Miroslav Radman and Robert Wagner, "The High Fidelity of DNA Duplication" *Scientific American*, Vol. 259, No. 2 (August 1988), p. 40.
2. Ashley Montagu, *Human Heredity* (NYC: The New American Library, 1963), p. 25.
3. George Howe, "Addendum to As a Watch Needs a Watchmaker," *Creation Research Society Quarterly*, Vol. 23, No. 2 (September 1986), p. 65.
4. Michael Denton, *Evolution: A Theory in Crisis* (Bethesda, Maryland: Adler and Adler Publishers, 1986), p. 338.
5. Fred Hoyle, *The Intelligent Universe*, quoted in *Nature*, 12 November, 1981.
6. Richard Lewontin, "Billions and billions of demons," *The New York Review*, January 9, 1997, p.31.
7. Homer Jacobson, "Information, Reproduction and the Origin of Life," *American Scientist*, January, 1955, p.121.
8. G. G. Simpson (1960) "The History of Life," in *Evolution of Life*, ed. Sol Tax (Chicago: University of Chicago Press), p. 135.
9. Francis Crick, *Life Itself* (New York: Simon and Schuster, 1981), p. 117–141.
10. Dawkins, Richard, *"River out of Eden: A Darwinian View of Life,"* Phoenix: London, 1996, pp.19-20.
11. J. E. Darnell, H.F. Lodish, and D. Baltimore, 1986 *Molecular Cell Biology*. New York: Scientific American Books.

12. Fred Holye and Chandra Wickramasinghe, *Evolution from Space*, London: J. M. Dent and Sons Co., 1981, p. 24.
13. A. E. Wilder-Smith, *The Illustrated Origins Answer Book* (Gilbert, AZ: Eden Communications, 1995), 25.
14. Michael Denton, *Evolution: A Theory in Crisis*, Bethesda: Adler & Adler, p. 338.

6

The Collapse of Evolution

> And God said, Let the Earth bring forth the living creature after his kind, cattle, and creeping thing, and beast of the Earth after his kind: and it was so (Genesis 1:24).

Notice that the Scriptures declare that species would reproduce after their own "kind." Despite the fact that the theory of evolution has been almost universally embraced by scientists, intellectuals, educators, and the media for over a century until quite recently, new scientific discoveries in the last two decades have revealed that evolution is now collapsing. Numerous secular books have been published in the last two decades by leading biologists, genetic researchers, and astronomers who have now rejected evolution as a theory that is unsupported by scientific evidence. As this chapter will demonstrate, numerous scientists have now finally admitted that they have accepted and taught evolution despite the lack of evidence primarily because the only logical alternative theory—Creation—was unacceptable.

One of the difficulties in understanding the truth about the theory of evolution is that we must clearly define and distinguish between *microevolution* and *macroevolution*. Microevolution describes the very small mutations and variations that scientists find over time that occur within species. These small genetic changes may lead to a variation of a species, such as birds that develop slightly larger beaks to adapt to changed environmental conditions. However, they still remain the original bird species. Cattle breeders use breeding techniques to develop cattle that yield more milk. However, they can never develop new tissues or organs.

For example, scientists have observed gradual changes in the breeds of cattle that farmers have purposely crossbred over decades to enhance the amount of lean meat or the amount of milk yield. Those who support Creation acknowledge that these small microevolutionary variations within a species obviously occur. Microevolutionary changes do not contradict the divine revelation in the Word of God that declares God's command recorded in Genesis 1:24: "Let the Earth bring forth the living creature after his kind." Slight microevolutionary change remains only a variation within the species and "after his kind" as affirmed by Scripture.

Macroevolution, however, is the general theory of evolution that claims untold random mutations somehow provide survival advantages over long periods, producing an entirely new species. The theory holds that these changes are reproduced generation after generation until the major changes actually produce an entirely new and different species that never before existed. While microevolution does exist, there is *no* scientific evidence to show that macroevolution occurs or has occurred, as this chapter will demonstrate.

Evolutionists Admit Flaws in Their Theory

As molecular genetics professor Michael Denton wrote in his book *Evolution: A Theory in Crisis*, many world-class biologists never fully accepted the validity of Darwin's theory of evolution. This is because its claims to explain biological diversity were clearly contradicted by the enormous complexity and ingenuity they discovered in their own research.[1]

Francis Hitching wrote *The Neck of the Giraffe: Where Darwin Went Wrong*, which documented that many evolutionary scientists concluded the theory of evolution was incompatible with their new knowledge of DNA and genetic complexity. Hitching said,

> Computer scientists, especially, were baffled as to how random mutations alone could possibly enrich the library of genetic information. A mutation, they repeatedly pointed out, is a mistake—the equivalent of a copying error. And how could mistakes build up into a new body of complicated ordered information?[2]

Scientists have never observed a single mutation

in the laboratory or in nature that adds information to an organism. Copying errors through mutation cannot possibly add new information, as the theory of evolution demands. Copying errors can only lose or corrupt information. Therefore, mutations cannot add information to generate positive change to an organism.

One of the most remarkable facts is that the theory of evolution depends entirely upon the unobserved and unproven assumption that random mutations over long periods of time will result in beneficial improvements in a species via added information that will be carried into future generations because they provide an enhanced opportunity for "survival of the fittest." However, scientific research contradicts this underlying assumption of evolution that accidental mutations could ever produce improvements in a species, let alone a transformation to an entirely new species.

As a result of the tremendous advances in the study of genetics, molecular biology, and the acknowledgement that the fossil record does not provide any support for the theory of evolution, a growing number of scientists have either publicly rejected evolution or have expressed very serious reservations about Darwin's theory. A small sampling of the growing number of books attacking evolution includes: *Darwin Retried; The Neck of the Giraffe: Where Darwin Went Wrong; The Great Evolution Mystery; The Bone Peddlers: Selling Evolution; Darwin Was Wrong—A Study in Probabilities; Darwinism: The Refutation of a Myth; Adam and Evolution; Darwin's Black Box;* and *Nature's Destiny*.

As Dr. Francis Hitching wrote, "A mutation was a pathological process that had nothing to do with evolution, and that the rare occasions when one proved helpful had been isolated flukes that did not constitute a general evolutionary mechanism." Hitching also acknowledged, "The first major objection to genes being the sole and sufficient driving force for evolution is that practically every mutation is obviously harmful, and puts the organism at a disadvantage rather than an advantage."[3]

The hidden truth that evolutionary scientists have seldom openly acknowledged is that mutations are genetic mistakes that fail to provide a logical answer to the question as to what fuels evolutionary development. In fact, mutations cannot possibly explain the biological diversity in our world. The problem is simply that mutations, by definition, are rare errors in the copying of the genetic code. They are genetic mistakes and, as a result, are almost always negative or neutral in their effect.

Hitching quoted evolutionist Theodosius Dobzhansky as admitting the problem with random mutations as a plausible explanation for the evolution of life. Dr. Dobzhansky wrote,

> A majority of mutations, both those arising in laboratories and those stored in natural populations, produce deteriorations of viability, hereditary disease, and monstrosities. Such changes, it would seem, can hardly serve as evolutionary building blocks.[4]

Biochemist Dr. Michael J. Behe, in his pivotal book, *Darwin's Black Box: A Biochemical Challenge to Evolution*, wrote about a significant survey of thirty biochemistry textbooks used in major universities throughout the world since 1965. Remarkably, the study revealed that a large majority of these biochemistry textbooks virtually ignored the subject of providing evidence supporting the theory of evolution, while several key textbooks did not mention evolution at all. In these textbooks, evolution at the molecular level was basically assumed to be true without the slightest attempt to provide evidence that evolution was either scientifically proven or certain. In fact, Professor Behe asserts that there are no authoritative scientific text books that attempt to prove that molecular evolution, a fundamental assumption of the theory of evolution, could ever have occurred through random chance mutations.[5]

Harold C. Urey, a winner of the Nobel Prize for chemistry, declared that many scientists now admit to the impossibility of evolution and that random mutations could never account for the remarkable biological diversity that characterizes life on Earth. However he also admitted that evolution was generally accepted by modern scientists as "an article of faith," as a kind of religious belief system, rather than as a result of a logical analysis of scientific facts. In confirmation of the actual religious nature of many scientists' acceptance of evolution, Professor Urey said,

> All of us who study the origin of life find that the more we look into it, the more we feel it is too complex to have evolved anywhere. . . . And yet we all believe as *an article of faith* that life evolved from dead matter on this planet. It is just that its complexity is so great that it is hard for us to imagine that it did.[6]

Another Nobel Prize winner, Ernest Chain, wrote about the failure of Darwin's theory of evolution.

To postulate that the development and survival of the fittest is entirely a consequence of chance mutations seems to me a hypothesis based on no evidence and irreconcilable with the facts. These classical evolutionary theories are a gross oversimplification of an immensely complex and intricate mass of facts, and it amazes me that they are swallowed so uncritically and readily, and for such a long time by so many scientists without a murmur of protest.[7]

The Real Motive for Supporting Evolution

In the last few decades, numerous scientists have publicly admitted that their real reason for accepting and promoting the theory of evolution is that, although the scientific evidence for macroevolution is non-existent, the only logical alternative was special Creation by God. Since that biblical alternative was absolutely unacceptable to their atheistic convictions, thousands of scientists chose to ignore the evidence they encountered in their own field that proved that chance and mutations could never explain the marvelous design and biological complexity that life displays.

Professor L. T. More, with the University of Cincinnati, spoke of the "faith" in evolution when he acknowledged the conflict between personal belief and scientific evidence: "Our faith in the doctrine of evolution depends upon our reluctance to accept the antagonistic doctrine of special creation." Professor More acknowledged the profound philosophical problem faced by scientists when they confronted the overwhelming problems now facing the theory of evolution,

> The reasonable view was to believe in spontaneous generation [evolution]; [for] the only alternative, is to believe in a single, primary act of supernatural creation. There is no third position. For this reason many scientists a century ago chose to regard the belief in spontaneous generation as a 'philosophical necessity.'[8]

Significantly, British astronomer Professor Fred Hoyle acknowledged that enormous problems existed with the theory of evolution. Hoyle actually admitted that the only reason the theory of evolution is still so widely accepted in the scientific community, despite the virtual lack of scientific evidence, is due to the need of atheistic people to deny the scientific evidence that God created the Universe. Remarkably, Professor Hoyle wrote that the theory of evolution survived despite the lack of scientific evidence because the theory is "considered socially desirable and even essential to the peace of mind of the body politic."[9]

Evolutionists Admit Living Organisms Appear to Be Designed

An Oxford University zoologist, Dr. Richard Dawkins, is one of many evolutionary scientists who have reluctantly admitted that they have a major problem in that everywhere they look they see abundant biological evidence that appears to be the result of intelligent design. Dawkins admitted this in his recent book *The Blind Watchmaker*: "Biology is the study of complicated things that give the appearance of having been designed for a purpose."[10] Professor Dawkins is so troubled by this evidence of deliberate design that he calls it a "powerful illusion." Dawkins wrote,

> The feature of living matter that most demands explanation is that it is almost unimaginably complicated in directions that convey a powerful illusion of deliberate design.[11]

Despite the awesome complexity of the information encoded within the DNA genetic code, Professor Francis Crick is determined to escape the obvious spiritual implications arising from this overwhelming new evidence of purposeful design. He advises biologists to remind themselves to ignore the evidence before their own eyes that complex biological forms are obviously the result of purposeful and intelligent design. "Biologists must constantly keep in mind that what they see was not designed, but rather evolved."[12]

This is an intriguing and very revealing statement by Professor Crick. In effect, Crick is telling scientists to ignore the evidence and the obvious logical implications regarding intelligent design that arise from scientific observation. This is "blind faith" in the religious theory of evolution in opposition to the biblical doctrine of God's Creation of the Universe and life itself.

The Collapse of Evolution

The theory of evolution suggests that all living things on Earth have come into being through accidental, random natural processes that began with a primeval mass of subatomic particles and radiation billions of years ago. Further, evolution states that life formed spontaneously from non-living inorganic matter and, through chance and random good mutations, life gradually evolved from a "simple" cell into the remarkable diversity of plant and animal life, as well as humanity. Evolution is taught as a fact, not as a theory, in the universities and high schools throughout the world. Although Charles Darwin popularized the theory almost one hundred and fifty years ago, it remains just that—a theory—because the scientific evidence required to prove it has never been found. This chapter will demonstrate that even evolutionists now admit there was never any fossil evidence that truly supported, let alone proved, the theory of evolution.

In fact, the scientific problems and inconsistencies of the theory of evolution are so overwhelmingly obvious that it now faces collapse on all fronts. The only thing holding the tattered theory of evolution together is the powerful desire of millions of people to hold on to the notion of evolution, regardless of its scientific weakness, because the alternative is unthinkable to its practitioners. The only logical alternative to evolution is obviously the theory that a supernatural being—God—purposefully designed and created the Universe and man. The idea of God as Creator ruled Western society for almost nineteen hundred years. However, during the last one hundred years, the almost universal acceptance of evolution by scientists, educators, intellectuals, and the media produced a widespread rejection of the Bible's authority and its claim in Genesis for God's special creation of life. These powerful groups created a virtual monopoly for the teaching of evolutionary theory in the last two generations, especially in the post-World War II generation.

A fascinating book entitled *The Intellectuals Speak out about God* astonished many readers with its revelations about recent scientific discoveries that totally disprove evolution. These leading scientists discuss numerous new scientific discoveries that support both the special creation of the Universe and the existence of God as the great Designer.

> Professor Stephen D. Schwarz explained that many of the latest discoveries of science have illustrated the impossibility that this complex Universe and life itself could ever have formed by random chance, no matter how old they assume the Universe is.

> Until quite recently it was thought by many people that the leading scientists universally support atheism, that science is the rational alternative to theism. However, it is now clear that science not only does not support atheism, but that it now lends rational support for theism. There is now strong scientific evidence for the existence of God. Scientists, without presupposing God or creation, without trying to prove them, have come up with findings that strongly

support the existence of God, His creation of the Universe and man, and supports a supernatural purpose for the world we live in.[13]

Scientific Reasons to Reject Evolution

There are several fundamental scientific reasons why the Universe and life itself could never have come into existence without a supernatural Creator.

Second Law of Thermodynamics

One of the most basic of all scientific observations is known as the Second Law of Thermodynamics. This fundamental law of science states that the total amount of usable energy throughout the Universe is constantly decreasing. In other words, the Universe is running down, which means the Universe is ultimately running out of its original usable energy. This law is fundamental in science because scientists have never found a single exception to this observation. The obvious conclusion is that the Universe must have been created at some point in time and has been running down ever since. This means the "steady state" theory of some early evolutionary scientists that the Universe has always existed is false.

In addition, since the Universe is running down, there must have been some point in the distant past when it began with the original totality of usable energy available—the moment of its beginning or creation. However, the first problem for evolution that must be faced is this: Where did the Universe and its massive energy come from and when did it begin? It is illogical to believe that the Universe accidentally came into existence out of nothing and out of random chance. The only logical conclusion is that the Universe was purposefully created with intelligent design and supernatural power by some Being who exists outside of the Universe, space, energy, and time itself. That Designer must be God.

Spontaneous creation of life

The second fundamental problem faced by the theory of evolution is the absolute impossibility that life was spontaneously generated by chance from inanimate or non-living inorganic elements. The evolutionists account for the chance development of life from non-living matter by imagining that the Earth's primitive oceans and atmosphere in the distant past (in a Universe without any life) were composed of an unusual chemical mixture they call "prebiotic soup." In other words, they suggest that the oceans and atmosphere on the primitive Earth were accidentally composed of every single one of the essential chemicals and that some energy source, possibly lightning, stimulated these unlikely chemicals to bond together over billions of years by pure chance to spontaneously generate life from non-living material. Although it appears to be virtually impossible that spontaneous generation of life could ever occur by blind chance without an intelligent designer or purpose, the evolutionist is forced to imagine that this actually occurred. Since he rejects the possibility of creation through a supernatural God, he is forced by his theory to accept the only other logical alternative—accidental spontaneous generation of life over billions of years.

Professor Chandra Wickramasinghe, an eminent

British scientist, describes the absolute impossibility that this prebiotic soup ever formed in the oceans and atmosphere of Earth by chance to create the possibility of life being spontaneously generated over millions of years. Professor Wickramasinghe concluded:

> One of the earliest questions that was raised in connection with the primordial soup was deciding whether at any early stage in the Earth's history, if there was a situation when the Earth's atmosphere was not of its present character, that is, it was *reducing* [without free oxygen] rather than *oxidizing*. We looked at this rather carefully, and we decided that the Earth's atmosphere was never of the right character to form an organic soup . . . we published this in a book under the title of *Lifecloud*. . . . Geochemists and geologists have now come round; they now go on to say that the primordial soup had to be imported from outside. . . . *There's no way it could have developed upon the Earth.* . . . The organic soup itself is not such a marvelous thing. It is a prerequisite for any biological activity to start; that's certainly true. But it doesn't follow that if you have an organic soup it could get life started. . . . And when we looked at the probabilities of the assembly of organic materials into a living system, it turns out that the improbabilities are really horrendous, horrific in extent and I concluded along with my colleague that [this] could not have happened spontaneously on the Earth. . . . *There's not enough*

time, there's not enough resources and there's no way in which that could have happened on the Earth.[14]

If the atmosphere contained free oxygen, as most scientists believe, then the oxygen would have combined with the amino acids, which would make them useless to the process. However, for the sake of argument, let us imagine that the impossible actually occurred by chance, producing this necessary prebiotic soup. But then what are the odds against the spontaneous generation of life developing accidentally from this "prebiotic soup"? Biologists have calculated that the odds against these chemicals spontaneously generating organic life by chance, according to Dr. Wickramasinghe, are only one chance in $10^{40,000}$. This number is 10 to the 40,000th power. The odds are equal to 1 followed by 40,000 zeros! It is a number so large that the human mind can scarcely conceive of it. To put this in perspective, scientists have calculated that the total number of atoms existing throughout the known Universe of 50 billion galaxies (each containing hundreds of millions of stars like our Milky Way) is only 10^{74}. That is 1 followed by 74 zeros.[15]

To illustrate, the odds against life being generated by chance from non-living matter are inconceivably less than your chance of locating one single target atom in a whole Universe of atoms by traveling blindfolded through the Universe in a spaceship. Imagining how an incredibly complex biological system such as humanity could ever evolve by chance belongs in the realm of pure fantasy, not science.

Biologists now know that the probability of life

being generated by chance out of non-living chemicals is a virtual impossibility. However, many evolutionary scientists argue that, no matter how statistically impossible evolution is, life *must* have formed from non-living matter by chance. Given billions of years, they argue that even the most statistically unlikely event might have occurred. However, this is purely blind faith in the religion of evolution. The truth is that the odds against life occurring spontaneously by chance are so enormous that it is far more likely that you will win a million dollar grand prize in the lottery every single night for the next ten thousand years!

A brilliant chemist and physicist, Professor Ilya Prigogine, winner of two Nobel Prizes in chemistry, has written that there is no possibility that life could ever have formed by random accident. "The statistical probability that organic structures and the most precisely harmonized reactions that typify living organisms would be generated by accident, is zero."[16]

Some Evolutionists Claim Life Came from Deep Space

Some of the evolutionary scientists who admit that life could never have spontaneously evolved on Earth have made a novel and extraordinary suggestion that either the prebiotic soup or lifeforms themselves evolved elsewhere and were brought to Earth in the distant past from another galaxy. They call this new and rather bizarre theory panspermia, as noted in a February 1992 article in the *Scientific American* magazine. However, this is not science; it is truly science fiction! If the mathematical probabilities make evolution impossible on Earth, as many evolutionists have finally acknowledged, then the same extraordinary odds make evolution impossible in any other galaxy or Universe, no matter how many billions of years scientists imagine they have.

This intellectual desperation of the scientists reveals two important facts. Evolution is finally collapsing due to the total absence of evidence in its favor and the insurmountable problems with the theory that life evolved by chance. Secondly, their desperation to accept any alternative variation in the theory to support evolution reveals their real motive for holding on to this discredited theory—their desire to escape the consequences of the alternative—the creation of life by a supernatural Creator—God.

Sir Fred Hoyle admitted that evolution could never have developed life by chance on our Earth, in our solar system, or in our Universe. Hoyle said, "For life to have originated on Earth it would be necessary that quite explicit instructions should have provided for its assembly."[17] After such an admission, you might expect that Sir Fred would graciously admit that there is a Creator. However, he claims that life was purposely "seeded" upon Earth in the distant past by some intergalactic space aliens who were themselves created in another galaxy by some superintelligent superbeing—a Higher Intelligence.

Hoyle's motive is to place the creative Higher Intelligence far away from us. He claims that the aliens that seeded life to Earth have a responsibility to serve the Higher Intelligence, but we, as a secondary lifeform, do not. Although he has been forced by the evidence to admit that there is an ultimate Creator, Hoyle deludes himself that he can escape his spiritual responsibility to serve and be accountable to God by inventing an entirely imaginary intermediate group of intergalactic aliens. In an article in *Newsweek* magazine in March, 1982, the editors realized that Hoyle now admitted a supernatural Creator; he just denied that humans needed to serve Him. *Newsweek* wrote, "Hoyle has actually performed the improbable feat of reinventing religion." Then the editor added that Hoyle was "led to exactly the same view that seemed prevalent in the Middle Ages: that life did not arise spontaneously on Earth."[18]

While most evolutionists admit that the odds against the origin of life by spontaneous generation and the probabilities against the accidental evolutionary development of life are truly astronomical, their basic assumption is that, given enough time, even those things that are extremely improbable will eventually happen. In other words, given the billions of years assumed to be available by the evolutionists, even the most unlikely events will eventually occur. But they are wrong. They don't really understand the implications of the laws of probability.

An example of this kind of evolutionary assumption is found in Dr. Richard Dawkins' book *The Blind Watchmaker.* Using the analogy of an alien being that lives for a hundred million years whom he presumed would have a quite different sense of time, Dawkins suggested that an extremely unlikely event, such as four bridge players each finding an extremely lucky hand of cards containing a perfect bridge hand (ace through king), would be something that a long-lived alien would not be especially surprised to witness. While a perfect bridge hand for four players—each one being dealt every single card of the thirteen cards needed (ace, 2, 3, 4, 5, 6, 7, 8, 9, 10, jack, queen, and king) would be extremely unlikely to occur within the lifetime of a regular human bridge player, Dawkins suggested that, if you lived long enough, even such an unlikely event would inevitably occur. Actually, Dawkins went further in his analogy. He suggested that such an alien living a hundred million years "will expect to be dealt a perfect bridge hand from time to time, and will scarcely trouble to write home about it when it happens."[19]

However, according to a brilliant analysis by Dr. Lee Spetner in his book *Not By Chance!*, it is possible to mathematically calculate the actual odds against the long-lived alien seeing a perfect bridge hand held by four players. And the odds are far more unlikely than the evolutionist Professor Dawkins imagines! Dr. Spetner demonstrated that

> if the alien plays 100 bridge hands every day of his life for 100 million years, he would play about 3.65×10^{12} hands. The chance of his seeing a perfect hand at least once in his life is then . . . about one chance in a quadrillion [one chance in a thousand billion]. That is less than Dawkins' chance of coming to New York for two weeks and winning the lottery twice in a row.[20]

In reality, the odds against evolution are far, far worse.

Monkeys Typing Shakespeare by Chance

The odds against the spontaneous generation of life and evolution itself are obviously astronomical. Scientists who support the theory of evolution often take the approach that, although the chances against evolution are absolutely staggering, even extremely improbable events are bound to happen one time given, billion of years. As George Wald wrote in his book, *Physics and Chemistry of Life*, the argument is often stated as:

> Given so much time the 'impossible' becomes possible, the possible probable, and the probable virtually certain. One has only to wait: time itself performs miracles.[21]

A common form of this argument is that "if you have a large enough number of monkeys typing away by chance at computer keyboards, they will eventually produce Shakespeare's plays." Surprisingly, the world's most prominent scientist, Professor Stephen Hawking, wrote in his book *A Brief History of Time: From the Big Bang to Black Holes* about this myth regarding monkeys and Shakespeare. Hawking wrote, "very occasionally by pure chance they will type out one of Shakespeare's sonnets."[22] Variations of this argument in favor of evolution have been used by Thomas Huxley, the great defender of Darwin, as well as Julian Huxley and Richard Dawkins. The reason this argument has been accepted by so many people is that most of us have difficulty fully comprehending extremely large or extremely small numbers.

A mathematical analysis of this probability problem was completed by Walter J. ReMine in his book *The Biotic Message: Evolution Versus Message Theory*. ReMine wrote,

> *The monkeys could not randomly type merely the*

first 100 characters of Hamlet. If we count only lowercase letters and spaces (27 characters in all), then the probability of typing the 100 characters is one chance in 27^{100} (one chance in 1.4×10^{143}). If each proton in the observable universe were a typing monkey (roughly 10^{80} in all), and they typed 500 characters per minute (faster than the fastest secretary), around the clock for 20 billion years, then all the monkeys together could make 5×10^{96} at the 100 characters. It would require an additional 3×10^{46} such universes to have an even chance at success. We scientifically conclude that the monkey scenario cannot succeed. For the scientist it would be perverse to insist otherwise.[23]

Many people have casually accepted the claim that "enough monkeys would eventually type a Shakespeare play by chance given enough time." However, the truth is that monkeys would never correctly type even a short sonnet of Shakespeare, let alone a complete play, no matter how many billions of years they were allowed to randomly type away at their keyboards. Most scientists consider that if the probability against an event occurring is greater than one million to one, then for all practical purposes the odds are *zero*. As the compelling evidence in this chapter confirms, the odds against the spontaneous generation of life and evolution itself are also *zero*.

Natural selection

Evolutionary scientists argue that natural selection provides the answer to why accidental chance mutations would result in the progressive evolution of life. The theory of natural selection requires progressive development at every successive step. However, random evolution and mutations cannot themselves possess intelligent understanding and planning. Unthinking evolutionary processes could never produce a half-formed eye as a transition in order to ultimately form a fully functioning eye. How could the complete eye have been produced by evolution through natural selection by step-by-step random mutations in gradual stages? Obviously, until the eye was fully formed and functional it was of no value whatsoever.

It seems that evolutionists, whether consciously or unconsciously, have regarded the blind and inanimate forces of the environment, or nature, as having the ability to create and think.[24]

In other words, despite their denial of intelligent design, the theory of evolution actually requires an intelligent, purposeful mind directing the process at every one of the supposed millions of imaginary intermediate stages as if these incremental changes were following a plan to produce a new lifeform.

Microevolution Limitations Imposed by DNA

Since 1908, scientists have performed genetic experiments on short-lived fruit flies (one month) to determine how to produce variations in the fruit flies such as to how small or large they could vary the wings. However, they constantly ran into an impenetrable wall that they could not overcome. The scientists could never cause real changes such as the development of a new ability, a new organ, or even a new structure that was truly new or different. Francis Hitching wrote a fascinating book entitled *The Neck of the Giraffe: Where Darwin Went Wrong*, in which he demonstrated that the genetic code had built-in safeguards and controls that severely limited genetic variations as part of an inherent fail-safe system to preserve the integrity of each species.

> In a remarkable series of experiments, mutant genes were paired to create an eyeless fly. When these flies in turn were interbred, the predictable result was offspring that were also eyeless. And so it continued for a few generations. But then, contrary to all expectations, a few flies began to hatch out with eyes. Somehow, the genetic code had a built-in repair mechanism that re-established the missing genes. The natural order reasserted itself. There are also built-in constraints. Plants reach a certain size and refuse to grow any larger. Fruit flies refuse to become anything but fruit flies under any circumstances yet devised. The genetic system, as its first priority, conserves, blocks, and stabilizes.[25]

In the nineteenth century, Georges Cuvier, a French anatomist, rejected the possibility of chance mutations resulting in the process of evolution. Cuvier wrote,

> All the organs of one and the same animal form a single system of which all the parts hold together, act and react upon each other; and there can be no modifications in any one of them that will not bring about analogous modification in them all.[26]

Cuvier explained the absolute impossibility of evo-lutionary change occurring within biological forms.

> Every organized being forms a whole . . . a pecu-liar system of its own, the parts of which mutu-ally correspond, and concur in producing the same definitive action, by a reciprocal reaction. None of these parts can change in form, without the others also changing.[27]

The Odds Against Chance Producing Hemoglobin

Dr. David Humphreys of McMaster University gave a speech at the University of Waterloo, Canada, on July 12, 1997, called "Evidence for a Creator" in which he suggested that conventional science has produced substantial evidence that the Universe, and hence life on Earth, was created by an intelligent, rational being. Dealing primarily with the evidence from chemistry and biology, Dr. Humphreys compared the theory of evolution, which suggests everything was produced by chance, against the theory that an intelligent being, namely God, created the Universe.

Dr. Humphreys suggests that it is statistically improb-able and unreasonable to assume that life was created by pure chance, given the statistical impossibility of life arising on Earth, and the tremendous complexity and diversity of biological lifeforms, even within the current estimated age of the Universe. As Professor Humphreys states, it is far more logical and consistent with the latest scientific evidence to conclude that the Universe and lifeforms were produced as a result of intelligent design. Dr. Humphreys noted that hemoglobin molecules in our blood are composed of twenty amino acids that occur in nature. These twenty amino acids could be arranged by random chance into a total of 10^{650} possible chemical combinations. However, only one of that nearly infinite number of possible combinations would produce the single correct complex hemoglobin molecule that is absolutely essential for the blood system of all animals and human beings. "The simultaneous formation of two or more molecules of this complexity is so improbable as to be inconceivable."[28]

Professor Chandra Wickramasinghe discussed his conclusions on the mathematical possibility of life forming in this theoretic prebiotic soup in the Earth's oceans and atmosphere through chance:

> And from the point of view of geo-chemistry and terrestrial experiments, if you look at the early Earth as a possible site for manufacturing life, it turns out that *the case is non-existent*, I would say, for such a thing happening on the Earth. . . . All that I am sure about is that *life could not have happened on the Earth spontaneously.*[29]

Professor Wickramasinghe declared that years of laboratory research has provided powerful evidence that the evolutionary theory of the development of biological life on Earth is simply impossible. This scientist concluded that complex biological life could never have formed by chance, even if we supposed that the necessary prebiotic soup actually existed on Earth. However, the evidence shows that the necessary prebiotic soup could never have formed. Furthermore, even if we suppose that a simple form of microorganism actually formed by chance (which has already been shown to be impossible), the evolution of that initial simple lifeform into the complex forms of insects, birds, and mammals is still impossible. Professor Wickramasinghe summarizes the absurdity of the theory of evolution:

> If you start with a simple micro-organism no matter how it arose on the Earth, primordial soup or otherwise, then if you just have that single organizational, informational unit and you said that you copied this sequentially time and time again, the question is, does that accumulate enough copying errors [mutations], enough mistakes in copying, and do these accumulations of copying errors lead to the diversity of living forms that one sees on the Earth? That's the general usual formulation of the Theory of Evolution . . . It's been claimed that the combination of the mistakes and the selection leads to the steady evolution of life. We looked at this quite systematically, quite carefully, in numerical terms. Checking all the numbers, rates of mutation and so on, we decided that there is no way in which that could even marginally approach the truth. On the contrary, any organized living system that developed or emerged say in the form of a microbe, 4 billion years ago, if it was allowed to copy itself time and time again, it would have destroyed itself essentially . . . *For every favorable mutation there will be hundreds of unfavorable mutations.*[30]

Aside from the obvious impossible odds against a

particular species developing by chance without intelligent design, we need to keep in mind that there are more than three million individual species of insects, together with tens of thousands of species of mammals, fish, reptiles, and birds. Remember, if the theory of evolution were true, every one of these millions of individual species would have needed, by random mutation, to beat the unimaginably large odds against the accidental evolution of its own species. To anyone who is willing to honestly look at these odds, it is obvious that the origin of the millions of species comprising the incredible biological diversity on Earth cannot be explained by the theory of evolution.

What About the Fossils?

There is no fossil evidence to support evolution. Many Christians and Jews who have been troubled by the claims of evolution will be astonished to discover that the evolutionists knew all along that there was *no* fossil evidence in support of evolution. Yet, many textbooks and teachers boldly declared that the fossils proved evolution to be true

After a century and a half of claims by evolutionists that just a little more time would produce the necessary fossil evidence of the missing links between species that would confirm the theory of evolution, we find there is an astonishing and *total lack of fossil evidence* to confirm any indisputable transitional forms, or "missing links," that must exist if the theory of evolution were actually scientifically true. However, in over one hundred and fifty years of a massive global search by scientists that has catalogued over one hundred million fossil specimens in museums and laboratories, they have failed to discover a single "missing link" fossil. If the evolutionists were intellectually honest, they would have abandoned evolution long ago.

In 1859, Charles Darwin acknowledged that the utter lack of fossil evidence for these missing links between one species and another provided "an unanswerable objection" to the theory of evolution. However, Darwin assumed that the search for fossils that would establish the truth of evolution was just beginning and that, given sufficient time and effort, scientists would soon discover the millions of transitional fossils required to prove that one species gradually transformed itself by natural selection into a new species.

Darwin himself was perplexed and very worried about the lack of fossil evidence. In his own words:

> Why, if species have descended from other species by fine gradations, do we not everywhere see innumerable transitional forms? Why is not all nature in confusion, instead of the species being, as we see them, well defined?. . . But, as by this theory innumerable transitional forms must have existed, why do we not find them embedded in countless numbers in the crust of the Earth?"[31]

He expressed his fears about his possible error in the following comments:

> I have asked myself whether I may not have devoted my life to a fantasy . . . I . . . am ready to cry with vexation at my blindness and presumption."[32]

Darwin admitted,

If it could be demonstrated that any complex organism existed which could not possibly have been formed by numerous, successive, slight modifications, my theory would absolutely break down.

He asked,

Why then is not every geological formation and every stratum full of such intermediate links? *Geology assuredly does not reveal any such finely graduated organic chain; and this, perhaps, is the most obvious and serious objection which can be urged against the theory.* The explanation lies, as I believe, in the extreme imperfection of the geological record.[33]

Darwin here sounds like a man reaching for straws. He had built his theory on imagined intermediate forms, but none of these forms had materialized during his lifetime. For the theory of evolution to be proven true, he needed to find these missing-link fossils. Rather than consider that his theory of evolution was false, he had to believe that the gradual evolutionary stages suggested by his theory would be discovered as more scientists searched and filled in the gaps in the fossil record. He honestly believed these fossils would eventually be found in the thousands, and prove his theory to be true beyond a doubt.

To date, though, every species discovered in the fossil record appears perfectly formed. Paleontologists have never discovered a fossil showing a partially formed species or a partially formed organ. Despite the fact that tens of thousands of scientists and millions of dedicated amateurs have been searching worldwide for these missing-link fossils to support evolution, *they have never found a single example.* The evidence is clear that there is no evidence of an evolutionary continuum. When the entire fossil record is carefully examined, we find that it reveals both extinct species and existing organisms with clearly defined gaps between them with *no* transitional forms. Every species appears in the fossil record as a perfect lifeform. This fossil record is precisely what you would expect to find if the Bible's account of God's special creation of the different species of life is true.

The late Dr. Stephen Jay Gould was an internationally-respected professor of geology and paleontology at Harvard University. He was a strong and eloquent supporter of evolution. However, he honestly admitted that the illustrations of evolutionary development found in the university science textbooks and television documentaries are actually fictitious inventions of creative artists that do not accurately represent scientific facts. He wrote the following statement in an article for *Natural History* magazine:

> The *extreme rarity* of transitional forms in the fossil record persists as the trade secret of paleontology. The evolutionary trees that adorn our textbooks have data only at the tips and nodes of their branches; the rest is inference, however reasonable, not the evidence of fossils. Yet Darwin was so wedded to gradualism that he wagered his entire theory on a denial of this literal record: The

geological record is extremely imperfect and this fact will to a large extent explain why we do not find interminable varieties, connecting together all the extinct and existing forms of life by the finest graduated steps. He who rejects these views on the nature of the geological record, will rightly reject my whole theory.[34]

Note that Dr. Gould's phrase "extreme rarity" is not quite accurate because the truth is that there are *no* transitional-form fossils. Professor Gould admitted that the claim of science textbooks that the fossil record supports evolution is false.

All paleontologists know that the fossil record contains precious little in the way of intermediate forms; transitions between major groups are characteristically abrupt."[35]

In other words, Dr. Gould admitted that the fossil record does not actually support the theory of gradual evolution (something that creationists have been claiming for many years). The new "punctuated equilibrium" theory states that evolution proceeded in rapid jumps that left no fossil evidence, followed by long periods with no changes.

Professor Gould also wrote,

The advent of the theory of punctuated equilibrium and the associated publicity it has generated have meant that for the first time biologists with little knowledge of paleontology have become aware of *the absence of transitional forms*.[36]

In other words, most scientists who believed evolution was proven by the fossils have only recently discovered that there are *no missing links* in the fossil record that point to evolution.

In May 1968, Professor Ronald West, Assistant Professor of Paleobiology at Kansas State University, wrote an article in the scientific journal *Compass* in which he made the following admission:

Contrary to what most scientists write, the fossil record does not support the Darwinian theory of evolution because it is this theory (there are several) which we use to interpret the fossil record. By doing so we are guilty of circular reasoning if we then say the fossil record supports this theory.[37]

Professor West confirmed what Dr. Stephen Gold and others have finally admitted—the hundreds of millions of fossils in the museums throughout the world do not support evolution at all. This fact, of course, is absolutely the opposite of what virtually every student in the Western world is taught during his or her science courses. We were constantly taught in science and biology courses in high school and college that the fossil record absolutely proves the truth of evolution, and therefore science totally contradicts the Bible's account of special creation as recorded in Genesis.

A scientific meeting in Chicago in 1980, "Conference on Macro-Evolution," produced a startling admission by some of the 120 participants regarding the nonexistence of fossil evidence supporting the essential "missing" links of evolution that Charles Darwin predicted would be found throughout the world. The world-famous paleontologist of the American Museum of Natural History, Dr. Niles Eldridge, stated at the conference, "The pattern that we were told to find for the last one hundred and twenty years does not exist."[38]

Professors D. Dewar and H. S. Shelton admitted the total failure of paleontologists to discover a single undisputed one of the billions of the supposed missing-link fossils representing transitional forms that would need to exist if the theory of evolution was actually true. In their book, *Is Evolution Proved?* Dewar and Shelton wrote, "Statistically, the absence of any traces of transitional forms proves that there never were any."[39] This remarkable conclusion regarding the total lack of any fossil evidence of "missing links" is also confirmed by Professor E. J. H. Corner in his book *Evolution in Contemporary Botanical Thought.*[40]

The "Archaeopteryx" Fossil

The evolutionists desperately point to a fossil, discovered in Austria, known as "archaeopteryx" (meaning "ancient wing"). They boldly claim that this archaeopteryx fossil provides absolute proof of at least one missing link, or transitional form, between reptiles and birds. However, despite the fact that this fossil displays a set of unusual teeth, everything else about the fossil reveals that *it is a true bird*, complete with fully-developed wings, feathers, and, probably, warm blood. Although the presence of teeth is unusual, this in no way proves that this fossil was partly a bird and partly a reptile or dinosaur, as the evolutionary textbooks now proudly declare. Some fossil birds display teeth and some reptiles have no teeth. God has produced some very strange creatures on this planet, including the duck-billed platypus, which has the bill of a bird and lays eggs but has the other characteristics of a mammal.[41]

The saga of the "dinosaur-bird" continues. In November 1999, *National Geographic* magazine published an article entitled *"Feathers for T. rex?"* written by its senior assistant editor, Christopher Sloan. The article included an amazing fictional illustration of a baby *Tyrannosaurus rex* with feathers. *National Geographic* boldly stated:

> We can now say that birds are theropods just as confidently as we say that humans are mammals.[42]

This assertion was immediately condemned by many leading scientists, including several top evolutionists. Professor Storrs Olson is the curator of birds at the National Museum of Natural History of the Smithsonian Institution in Washington, D.C. Dr. Olson wrote:

> *National Geographic* has reached an all-time low for engaging in *sensationalistic, unsubstantiated, tabloid journalism.* . . . It eventually became clear to me that National *Geographic* was not interested in anything other than the prevailing dogma that birds evolved from dinosaurs.[43]

Information has been published that reveals that this second "feathered dinosaur" fossil was illegally exported from Liaoning Province in China. Finally, it was revealed that the entire fossil is a hoax and a fraud. Although the evolutionists at *National Geographic* called

it a "true missing link in the complex chain that con-
nects dinosaurs and birds," it has now been revealed
as a fraudulently designed combination of two distinct
and totally unrelated fossils. The "feathered dinosaur"
displayed in *National Geographic* is actually composed of
a birdlike upper torso combined with the feet and tail of
a small dinosaur known as a raptor. This scientific fiasco
is a warning to all that we should treat the major media
claims regarding evolution with great skepticism, as the
media are overwhelmingly predisposed to support and
publicize any information that supports the theory of
evolution or will sell on the newsstand.

Evolution's Great Lie:
The "Ascent of Man", the Famous Series of
Ape-men Illustrating Human Evolution

But what about the famous fossils found around the
world that purportedly show the evolutionary "ascent
of man" from primitive ape-man to his ultimate succes-
sor—the evolutionary scientist carrying his briefcase
into a university? Most of us have listened to professors,
watched television documentaries, or read Time-Life
books illustrating and declaring authoritatively that we
are all descended from primitive ape-men. As difficult
as it is to believe, the scientific evidence is now overwhelmingly in support of the conclusion that the entire
"ascent of man" from ape-man to modern humans is
one of the greatest scientific frauds in history. Hundreds
of millions of students around the world have been
taught a terrible lie to convince them that science has
absolutely proven that evolution is true and that the

Bible's account of Creation must therefore be logically rejected as unscientific and false.

One of the most effective techniques developed by atheists to convince the average person that the evolutionary theory is true is the constant referral to the discovery of a series of hominid ape-men fossils that were found around the globe during the last 150 years. These "missing link" ape-men creatures supposedly demonstrated the gradual evolution over millions of years from primitive ape-like creatures to modern men. The evolutionists confidently presented each of these new discoveries as the long-promised missing links that demonstrate the evolutionary transition from our ancient ancestors, an ape-like creature, to the modern *Homo sapiens. (See picture section, figure 14.)*

However, a detailed examination of the actual record of human fossils reveals a remarkable account of scientific fraud, mistaken identification, and outright misrepresentation. Few readers of these "scientific" accounts of evolutionary discoveries of ape-men in the popular press realize that these so-called hominids' fossil skeletons often consist of little more than a single tooth, a jaw fragment, a quarter-sized part of a skull, or a portion of an elbow or knee joint. From this sparse material, the scientists and their willing accomplices, the evolutionary textbook artists, and museum curators, create an imaginary illustration of a complete ape-man. These cavemen illustrations are then accepted by the vast majority in our Western culture as convincing scientific proof that modern man developed over great periods of time by gradual transitions from ape-like ancestors. However, a careful examination of the actual scientific evidence reveals that this presentation of the evolution of man is purely science fiction, based solely upon their underlying evolutionary presuppositions and the atheistic bias of the scientists.

In fact, some of these "discoveries" of small bone fragments and teeth were actually found far away from the other bone fragments that they subsequently placed together to create a complete new "hominid" fossil skeleton. Other major "discoveries" of so-called ape-man fossils were proven subsequently to be the bones of pigs, donkeys, or apes. Let us examine each of these discoveries and see where the truth lies.

Many of These Ape-Man "Missing Links" are Apes or Pigs

An analysis of the "missing link" evidence that supposedly demonstrates the evolutionary development of man from ape-like ancestors includes a number of supposed hominid ape-men presented by paleontologists as evidence of the gradual evolutionary transition from primitive ape-like ancestors to man. However, research has now shown that most of these examples of "so-called" ape-men are really extinct forms of apes, monkeys, pigs, or horses, and have no relationship whatsoever to ancient or modern humans. Significantly, the majority of the "missing link" fossil specimens that are now proven to be extinct apes or monkeys were found in geographic areas where ape and monkey skeletons are found in abundance. Bone fragments are often deformed by the common diseases experienced by people in past centuries, including rickets, starvation, Paget's disease, syphilis, and arthritis.

Many so-called humanoid "missing links" have now been proven to be fossils of either monkeys, apes or even misidentifications of the ancient teeth of pigs and horses.

Piltdown Man I and II

Occasionally, these so-called ape-man discoveries were revealed years later to be complete hoaxes, and such is the case of the infamous Piltdown Man that was discovered at the Piltdown quarry in England in June 1912. This gravel pit is located approximately forty miles south of London in east Sussex, only a few miles west of the battleground of the famous Battle of Hastings. This "discovery" was made by a lawyer, Charles Dawson, who was an amateur geologist whose previous fossil discoveries had been accepted by the British Museum in London.

Unfortunately, this fossil, known as the "Piltdown Man," laid the foundation for millions of educated people to accept the false theory of the evolution of modern humans descending from ancient ape-like ancestors. Several years later, in 1917, after Dawson's death, it was claimed that he had discovered another fossilized skull, known as Piltdown Man II. This "discovery" was so helpful to those who supported evolution that it was rapidly and unquestionably accepted by scientists and intellectuals throughout the world for the next four decades.

Finally in 1953, forty-one years later, a detailed examination of the skull fragments of the famous Piltdown

Man skull using a test based on fluoride absorption proved that someone had purposely and fraudulently planted a modern human skull fragment on top of the jaw of an orangutan in the original Piltdown quarry. An article in October 1956 in the *Reader's Digest* recounted the new evidence from a scientific article entitled "The Great Piltdown Hoax" that earlier appeared in the *Popular Science Monthly*. The instigator of this evolutionary plot dyed the teeth and skull fragments with the chemical bichromate of potash to convince other scientists that the skull was extremely old. Malcolm Bowden wrote in his book, *Ape-Men: Fact or Fallacy*, that the evidence points toward the fact that the forger was none other than the famous Jesuit philosopher and evolutionist Pierre Teilhard de Cardin.[44] Professors Stephen J. Gould and Louis Leakey have both written about their conviction that Pierre Teilhard de Cardin was the one who created the scientific fraud of the Piltdown Man.

Despite the Piltdown Man being a scientific hoax, the damage was done. Hundreds of university researchers and scientists wrote hundreds of doctoral treatises about the Piltdown Man as the direct ancestor of modern man during the decades between its "discovery" in the quarry and its final determination as a fraud in 1953.

Ramapithecus

Another supposedly important hominid fossil discovery in 1932 from India and Africa is known as *Ramapithecus*, which was presented by evolutionists as the primary missing link between apes and humans for nearly fifty years. However, few people understood that the whole imaginary skeleton of *Ramapithecus* was based solely on a few fossilized teeth. Unfortunately for the evolutionary theory, scientists later closely examined the teeth and discovered that they were actually the teeth of a modern orangutan, not the teeth of an evolutionary ape-man. *Ramapithecus* is now totally rejected by evolutionists.[45]

Java Man

In 1891, convict workers employed by Dr. Eugene Dubois found on the island of Java (Indonesia) in the south Pacific several fossilized bone fragments. He identified these fossils as a 750,000-year-old man, *Homo erectus*. Dr. Dubois's identification was based on the fact that the skeleton fragments suggested to him that the individual walked erect as a humanoid, unlike an ape. However, the only evidence for this important ape-man fossil was a skull cap fragment, three molar teeth, and a bone fragment from a thighbone. However, the thighbone fragment was identical to a thighbone of a modern human skeleton.

Strangely, Dr. Dubois did not initially admit that the Java Man skull cap they discovered was not found near the other bone fragments but rather found forty-six feet away from the other bones. There is no rational reason to conclude that this skull cap was ever part of an initial skeleton connected to the other bone fragments found over a seventy-foot area during approximately one year of digging completed by untrained workers.

An example of the weakness of this claimed ape-man evidence for the evolutionary development of man is found in the words of Professor Virchow, who wrote: "There is no evidence at all that these bones were part of the same creature."[46] Unfortunately, most of these original Java Man bones have now been lost. The scientists somehow neglected to inform the public that they had also discovered the skeletal remains of ten modern human skeletons at the very same site, together with tools, etc., indicating that this collection of fossilized bones was actually the remains of modern humans, not some imaginary ancient ape-men.

Nebraska Man

My personal favorite fictional character in the imaginary evolutionary group of ape-men is the so-called Nebraska Man. Professor Harold Cook discovered his "remains" in 1922 in the western portion of Nebraska. The head of the American Museum of History, Dr. Henry F. Osborn, confidently announced that this ape-man was the long-sought evidence of the missing link between ancient chimpanzees, Java Man, and modern man. Detailed drawings of this illustrious ape-man ancestor (and his wife!) carrying his club were printed in various publications, including the *Illustrated London Times*, in 1922. However, the artists had to create the entire skeleton, muscles, face, skull, and hair of Nebraska Man out of pure imagination. It was a complete fraud.

Astonishingly, the only evidence the scientists actually found was *a single fossilized tooth*. The scientific illustrator created his drawings of this ancient and supposed primitive ape-man and his family based on nothing more than pure artistic imagination and the desire to draw an ancient caveman. Virtually everyone who would observe such a drawing would naturally believe that the discovered fossil remains must have actually supported such an artistic re-creation. The punch-line to this sad evolutionary joke is that the single fossil tooth that composed the sole real evidence of Nebraska Man finally turned out to not even be human, but the tooth of an extinct *pig*.[47]

The famous 1925 Scopes evolution trial was held in Dayton, Tennessee, over the issue of whether a teacher had violated the Tennessee law of that time against teaching the theory of evolution in their schools. Unfortunately, the vast majority of people have learned of this important trial solely through the famous movie that totally manipulated the truth of the court record. The movie persuaded millions that those who supported biblical Creation were intellectually bankrupt. The historic truth is that the teacher who violated the Tennessee law against teaching evolution lost the case. The so-called "Nebraska Man" was a powerful part of the evidence appealed to by the famous atheist lawyer Clarence Darrow as compelling proof that the evolution of man from primitive ape-man was credible science. William Jennings Bryan, the lawyer for the state of Tennessee, was intimidated by Clarence Darrow's repeated appeal to the so-called evidence from the Nebraska Man fossil, claiming that evolution was demonstrated by the fossil evidence. However, as detailed above, the Nebraska Man was nothing more than a fictional invention created by evolutionary scientists from a tooth of an ancient pig.

While the Nebraska Man was a fraud, it was matched by another evolutionary discovery, the Southwest Colorado Man, which shared the distinction of being built upon the sole evidence of another ancient fossilized tooth. Unfortunately for the evolutionists, this tooth also turned out to be something less than evidence for an ape-man. The Southwest Colorado Man was based solely upon another tooth, but this time of an ancient horse.

Lucy

A new missing-link, known as Lucy, was found in northern Ethiopia in 1974 and supposedly provided powerful evidence of another link in the evolution of man. The scientists, led by Professor Richard Leakey, announced that Lucy was three-and-a-half feet high, walked erect as a hominid, and lived over three million years ago. Lucy was described as an early ancestor of modern humans. They catalogued Lucy as *Australopithecus afarensis*, and claimed she was an early human because the knee-joint proved that this individual walked upright.

Further digging at the Lucy site found fossilized bones of extremely ape-like creatures with chimpanzee-sized forearms that made it very probable that these creatures walked on four feet as opposed to the erect posture that characterizes humans.[48] One of the most famous paleontologists is Richard Leakey, the son of the eminent evolutionary scientists Louis and Mary Leakey. Richard Leakey identified Lucy as a hominoid, a definite ancestor of mankind. However, Richard Leakey admitted that the paleontologists are often working from their imagination more than from the actual fossil evidence, which is usually so meager. Dr. Leakey admitted,

> Our task is not unlike attempting to assemble a three-dimensional jigsaw puzzle in which most of the pieces are missing, and those few bits which are at hand are broken![49]

Some scientists have candidly admitted that their preconceived opinions in favor of evolution govern to a great degree the conclusions they reach about the nature of the fossil evidence. Dr. Gareth Nelson, of the American Museum of Natural History, admitted this in the following statement. "We've got to have some ancestors. We'll pick those. Why? Because we know they have to be there, and these are the best candidates. That's by and large the way it has worked. I am not exaggerating."[50] In other words, the theory of evolution required a series of missing-link ape-men, and the scientists interpreted the fossil evidence to support their theory.

The Last Three "Missing Links" are Actually Human Skeletons

The last three "missing links" presented by evolutionists have recently been proven to be fossil remains of modern humans revealing no significant differences from our modern human skeletons. These three modern human skeletons were discovered in areas where monkeys and apes probably never existed. These three fossilized remains—Peking Man, Neanderthal Man, and

Cro-Magnon Man—have now been proven to belong to modern humans.

Many of these hominid skulls were originally believed to be ancient ape-men because the scientists in the first half of the last century did not know that the normal range of size for modern human skulls included the smaller skulls of these so-called ape-men. Scientists have now found that recently deceased human skeletons throughout the world differ markedly in the size of the skull and various bones, but they are still modern humans. There is a fairly wide range of skull sizes found in modern humans, which accounts for the differences discovered in the skull fragments that scientists previously concluded belonged to a primitive ape-man.

Homo erectus: *Peking Man*

The name *Homo erectus* refers to the fact that the evidence reveals that Peking Man walked erect. The only reason evolutionists suggested this skeleton was a subhuman rather than a modern man was the fact that this particular specimen had a somewhat smaller skull than some modern humans. However, it has now been proven that the size of *Homo erectus*'s brain was actually equal to the average size of most European men today. Therefore, there is no scientific reason whatsoever to believe that this Peking Man fossil represents anything other than a modern human skeleton that adds nothing to the evidence that purports to support the theory of the evolution of man. All of these fossils relating to Peking Man have disappeared

Neanderthal Man

Neanderthal fossils of the skull of a man were discovered in the Neander Valley in Germany. The discovery of these fossils convinced millions that scientists had now proven the theory of the evolution of man from ape-like ancestors. However, further research has revealed that Neanderthal Man was actually a modern man. An analysis of the deformed skull revealed that this deformity was caused by a disease called *Arthritis deformans*. In fact, Neanderthal Man turned out to be a fairly recent human skeleton of a man who also suffered severely from a Vitamin D deficiency. This Vitamin D deficiency produced the disease known as rickets, which accounted for the unusual ridges over the eyebrows and his curved leg bones.

Most people who were taught the theory of evolution in high school still believe that modern humans are descended from cavemen ancestors with heavy ridges on their eyebrows. However, not one of the other fossilized skeletons in the supposed evolutionary series has demonstrated these heavy brow ridges.

> Scientists have concluded that all of the so-called *primitive* features of Neanderthal people were due to pathological conditions, or diseases.[51]

Neanderthal skeletons are now officially classified scientifically as *Homo sapiens neanderthalensis*, in other words, as normal humans. Interestingly, these Neanderthal men possessed skulls with a brain that is actually larger than the brains of most humans alive today.

Cro-Magnon Man

The fossil identified as Cro-Magnon Man is indistinguishable from modern man. The sole reason evolutionists suppose this fossil was that of a primitive ape-man was that it was found near a series of cave drawings that were considered primitive. This identification as an ape-man is no longer supported by modern scientists, and Cro-Magnon Man is no longer considered as a primitive ancestor of modern man.

The Conclusion from Fossil Records

The final result of this analysis of these famous ape-man "missing links" is that the evidence supporting human evolution simply does not exist. The evolutionary scientists have failed to find a single genuine transitional form between ape-like ancestors and men, despite their constant search during the last 150 years. The museums and universities have more than 100 million fossils collected from every area on Earth during the last century and a half. The truth is this: There is *no* fossil evidence that supports the evolutionary theory of the gradual development of life from simple to complex forms, including humans.

The Latest Evolutionary Retreat: Punctuated Evolution

Many evolutionary scientists have finally admitted that the fossil record provides no real fossil evidence whatsoever of the millions of gradual transitional steps or "missing links" required by evolutionary theory.

However, they are now proposing a new theory of evolution called "punctuated evolution." This new theory claims that there is no evolutionary change in a species for millions of years and then, suddenly, these animals change spontaneously to a new species in one leap within a single generation without any gradual or transitional process. They claim that this is why there is no fossil evidence for evolution.

This recent modification of Darwin's theory is, in fact, a total repudiation of his theory of gradual, accumulated changes over millions of years of uniform processes. The real motivation behind their new theory of punctuated evolution is their growing embarrassment that no fossil evidence has *ever* been found that demonstrates gradual transitions from simple forms to more complex forms of animals or plants. According to this new theory, this rapid change in one generation accounts for evolution taking place without any evidence existing for gradual change being found in the fossil record. This is not science—it is nothing less than science fiction. This new theory is a vain attempt to explain the fact that *none* of the data in the fossil record provides evidence in support of the theory of evolution. I believe we can easily dismiss this unscientific and ridiculous twist on the evolution theory.

Notes

1. Michael Denton, *Evolution: A Theory in Crisis*, London: Burnett Books, 1985, p. 326–329.
2. Francis Hitching, *The Neck of the Giraffe: Where Darwin Went Wrong*, London: Pan Books, 1982.
3 . Francis Hitching, *The Neck of the Giraffe: Where Darwin Went Wrong*, London: Pan Books, 1982.
4. Francis Hitching, *The Neck of the Giraffe: Where Darwin Went Wrong*, London: Pan Books, 1982.
5. Michael J. Behe, *Darwin's Black Box*, New York: The Free Press, 1966. p. 182-183.
6. Harold C. Urey, *Christian Science Monitor*, January 4, 1962 (italics added).
7. Ernest Chain, "Was Darwin Wrong" *Life Magazine*, April 1982.
8. L. T. More, *The Dogma of Evolution,* Princeton: Princeton University Press.
9. Fred Hoyle and Chandra Wickramasinghe, *Evolution from Space*, London: J. M. Dent and Sons Co., 1981, p. 148.
10. Richard Dawkins, *The Blind Watchmaker* [1986], Penguin: London, 1991, reprint, p. 1.
11. Richard Dawkins, Zoologist and Professor for the Public Understanding of Science, Oxford University, "Darwin Triumphant: Darwinism as a Universal Truth," in Robinson M. H. & Tiger L., eds., *Man & Beast Revisited*, Smithsonian Institution Press: Washington DC, 1991, p. 24).
12. F. H. C. Crick, *What Mad Pursuit: A Personal View of Scientific Discovery* [1988], Penguin Books: London, 1990, reprint, p. 138.

13 Roy Abraham Varghese, ed., *The Intellectuals Speak Out About God* (Chicago: Regnery Gateway, 1984), p. 100-103.

14. Chandra Wickramasinghe, *The Intellectuals Speak out about God* (Chicago: Regnery Gateway, 1984), 25-26.

15. Chandra Wickramasinghe, *The Intellectuals Speak out about God* (Chicago: Regnery Gateway, 1984), 26.

16. I. Prigogine, N. Gregair, A. Babbyabtz, *Physics Today* 25, p. 23–28.

17. Fred Hoyle and Chandra Wickramasinghe, *Evolution from Space*, London: J. M. Dent and Sons Co., 1981, p. 30

18. *Newsweek*, March, 1982.

19. Richard Dawkins, *The Blind Watchmaker*, London: W. W. Norton. 1986.

20. Lee Spetner, *Not By Chance!* New York: The Judaica Press, 1998, p. 166.

21. George Wald, 1955 (New York: Simon & Schuster,1955), p. 12.

22. S. W. Hawking, 1988, *A Brief History of Time: From the Big Bang to Black Holes*, p. 123.

23. Walter J. ReMine, 1993, *The Biotic Message: Evolution Versus Message Theory*, St. Paul Science: Saint Paul, Minnesota (USA), p: 80.

24. B. G. Ranganathan, *Origins?* Carlisle: The Banner of Truth Trust, 1988, p. 11.

25. Francis Hitching, *The Neck of the Giraffe: Where Darwin Went Wrong*, London: Pan Books, 1982, pp. 57, 61.

26. George Cuvier, *Researches sur les ossements fossiles de quadrupedes, Discors preliminaire*, English trans. by R. Kerr (1813), entitled Essay on the Theory of the Earth (Edinburgh and London), pp. 94–95.

27. George Cuvier, (1829) *Revolutions of the Surface of the Earth* (London: Whittaker, Treacher & Arnot), p. 60.

28. David Humphreys, *Imprint News,* July 26, 1996, Volume 19, Number 7.

29. Chandra Wickramasinghe, *The Intellectuals Speak out about God* (Chicago: Regnery Gateway, 1984), pp. 25–29.

30. Chandra Wickramasinghe, The *Intellectuals Speak Out About God,* (Chicago: Regnery Gateway, 1984), 29.

31. Charles Darwin, *The Origin of Species* (London: J. M. Dent & Sons Ltd., 1971).

32. Herbert Wendt. *From Ape to Man* (New York: The Bubbs Merril Co., 1972), p. 59.

33. Charles Darwin, *The Origin of Species,* (London: J. M. Dent & Sons Ltd., 1971), 292-293 (italics added).

34. Stephen Jay Gould, *Natural History* (May 1977): 14.

35. Stephen Jay Gould, *Natural History* 86(6): 22-30 (1977).

36. Stephen J. Gould, *The Panda's Thumb,* New York: W. W. Norton and Co., p. 181 (italics added).

37. Ronald R. West, *Compass,* vol. 45, (1968): 216.

38. Francis Hitching, *The Neck of the Giraffe: Where Darwin Went Wrong* (New York: Ticknor and Fields, 1982) p. 22.

39. D. Dewar and H. S. Shelton, *Is Evolution Proved?,* Hollis and Carter, 1947.

40. E. J. H. Corner, *Evolution in Contemporary Botanical Thought*, A.M. MacLeod and L. S. Cobley, eds., Chicago: Quadrangle Books, 1961.

41. Internet: Dr. David Menton, Associate Professor of Anatomy, http://www.answersingenesis.org/docs/1352.asp

42. Sloan, C. P., "Feathers for *T. Rex*?" *National Geographic* 196(5):98–107, November 1999.

43. S. L. Olsen, Letter to: Dr. Peter Raven, Secretary, Committee for Research and Exploration, National Geographic Society.

44. Malcolm Bowden, *Ape-Men: Fact or Fallacy* (Bromley, Kent: Sovereign Publications, 1977), p. 3-47.

45. Duane T. Gish, *Evolution: The Fossils still say No!*, (El Cajon, CA.: Institute For Creation Research, 1995): 326.

46. W. A. Criswell, *Did Man Just Happen?*, Zondervan Publishing Co., Grand Rapids, Michigan, 1973, p. 85.

47. Duane T. Gish, *Evolution: The Fossils Still say No!*, (El Cajon, CA.: Institute For Creation Research, 1995): 326.

48. *Nature*, 368:449–451 1994.

49. Internet site: http://emporium.turnpike.net/c/os/evid4.htm

50. Garth Nelson, *Lucy's Child*, (New York: William Morrow and Co., 1989): 74.

51. Duane T. Gish, *The Amazing Story of Creation from Science and the Bible*, (El Cajon, CA: Institute for Creation Research, 1990): 81.

Chapter 7

7

Intellectuals Question Evolution

In the light of the overwhelming new scientific evidence that evolution is no longer supported by the discoveries of fossils and that evolution is now known to be mathematically impossible, the average reader must wonder why the theory of evolution through random, blind mutations and natural selection has survived for so long as a universally taught theory. I believe the answer lies in the strong desire by many scientists and educators to escape the consequences of the only logical alternative to evolution--a belief in God as our Creator and the truth that each of us has an appointment to meet our Creator God as our judge following our death.

Two thousand years ago, the Apostle Paul wrote to

his disciple Timothy and prophesied that in the last days before Christ's return to establish His kingdom, men would arise who would purposely deny the truth about God's creation of the Universe and would invent a new theory that would eliminate God and invent "fables" to explain the existence of the world and humanity.

> For the time will come when they will not endure sound doctrine; but after their own lusts shall they heap to themselves teachers, having itching ears; and they shall turn away their ears from the truth, and shall be turned unto fables (2 Timothy 4:3-4).

Paul described these future atheistic teachers as

> ever learning, and never able to come to the knowledge of the truth (2 Timothy 3:7).

Supporters of the theory of evolution understand very clearly that, if evolution is proven to be false, then the only possible logical alternative explanation for the existence of this Universe and the complexity of life is that there is a God who has created us. This alternative to evolution is so unthinkable and unacceptable to many scientists and intellectuals that they desperately hold onto the faltering theory of evolution to their dying day, despite the total absence of scientific evidence to support it.

Evolutionary scientist Arthur Keith admitted,

> Evolution is unproved and unprovable. We believe it only because the only alternative is special creation which is unthinkable.[1]

In reality, these scientists actually demonstrate their own "blind faith" in their scientific religion of evolution and consequently ignore any evidence that contradicts their faltering theory. Their realization of the scientific weakness of the case for evolution is the real reason evolutionists are so determined to keep the theory of special creation from ever being taught as an alternate theory, together with evolution, in schools and universities. Evolution can only survive in the arena of public opinion if no one is allowed to challenge it with the scientific facts that point to special creation as a more sound theory.

Some evolutionists are honest enough to admit that their support for evolution is actually a matter of religious faith as opposed to empircal science. Professor G. A. Kerkut, of the University of Southampton (London), expressed his conclusion regarding the underlying attitudes of many scientists on the subject of biogenesis (evolution):

> It is therefore a *matter of faith* on the part of the biologist that biogenesis [evolution] did occur and he can choose whatever method of biogenesis happens to suit him personally; the evidence for what did happen is not available.[2]

In other words, forget about scientific evidence, just *believe* in evolution as a "matter of faith" because the evidence "is not available."

Dr. Henry Morris was originally a firm believer in evolution until he began to examine the evidence critically for himself. He soon realized that the whole theory was not supported by scientific evidence at all, but that evolution had actually become a new scientific religion for those who wished to escape the consequences of the truth of the Bible's claims about Creation, a personal God, salvation, and our ultimate judgment before our God. He said,

> Many . . . believe in evolution for the simple reason that they think science has proven it to be a 'fact' and, therefore, it must be accepted. . . . In recent years, a great many people . . . having finally been persuaded to make a real examination of the problem of evolution, have become convinced of its fallacy and are now convinced anti-evolutionists.[3]

In the last decade, numerous evolutionists have admitted in print that the actual scientific evidence found in the fossil record does not really support the theory of evolution. Many scientists have acknowledged that they have not found any evidence whatsoever in the fossil record of animals with partially developed limbs or organs such as partial legs, brains, or eyes. Yet if their theory of evolution is true, the fossil record should contain millions of such examples of transitional missing links and partially developed organs. However, not one such fossil has *ever* been found.

Admissions By Scientists That Evolution Is Not Supported By Evidence

A strong supporter of the theory of evolution, Professor T. L. Moor, wrote,

The more one studies paleontology, the more certain one becomes that evolution is based on faith alone.[4]

Dr. Niles Eldredge has written,

We paleontologists have said that the history of life supports (the story of gradual adaptive change), all the while really knowing that it does not."[5]

Another evolutionist, Dr. Solly Zuckerman, finally admitted the truth when he wrote,

The record of reckless speculation of human origins) is so astonishing that it is legitimate to ask whether much science is yet to be found in this field at all.[6]

None of us come to the time and place of examining a personal philosophical decision empty-handed. Each of us has a lifetime of reading, teaching, and conversation invested in our fundamental worldview. Where we stand on an issue depends to a great degree on where we sit. Therefore, it is very difficult for any of us to abandon a philosophy or viewpoint that we have embraced for most of our adult life. This is why so many scientists and intellectuals have found it so hard to honestly evaluate the discoveries in the last half century that have destroyed the scientific foundations of the theory of evolution. It is also true that the bias against God's creation within the academic community is so strong that many scientists and professors fear that any wavering regarding their support for evolution would seriously hurt their career and ability to win financial grants for research from governments and foundations.

The world has seen almost a century and a half of virtually universal support for the materialistic theory of evolution by scientists, educators, and intellectuals throughout the world. However, the recent scientific discoveries in astronomy, the nature of the atom, the staggering complexity of the DNA genetic code, and the utter failure to find fossil evidence for missing links have motivated many scientists to finally abandon the theory of evolution. An article in *Science Digest Special* noted that an increasing number of scientists are privately or publicly rejecting the atheistic materialism and evolutionary theory that was previously the fundamental tenet of western science.

> Scientists who utterly reject Evolution may be one of our fastest-growing controversial minorities. . . . Many of the scientists supporting this position hold impressive credentials in science.[7]

Many evolutionary scientists now accept that the mathematical odds against life ever forming by random chance from inanimate matter are totally impossible. Dr. Harold Urey, a Nobel Prize-winner for his research in chemistry, wrote about the impossibility that evolution could be true, but still admitted he believed in evolution despite the utter lack of scientific evidence supporting this theory.

> All of us who study the origin of life find that the more we look into it, the more we feel that it is too complex to have evolved anywhere.

Incredibly, Dr. Urey then added these words,

We believe as an article of faith that life evolved from dead matter on this planet. It is just that its complexity is so great, *it is hard for us to imagine that it did.* (Italics added.)[8]

His honest admission proved that his acceptance of evolution was not based on logic or scientific evidence, but on blind faith.

At the Alpach Symposium conference, where scientists dealt with the growing problems with the theory of evolution, one of the speakers admitted that the reason evolution was still strongly supported by intellectuals, the education establishment, and the media had nothing to do with whether it was true or false. "I think that the fact that a theory so vague, so insufficiently verifiable and so far from the criteria otherwise applied in 'hard' science has become a dogma can be explained only on sociological grounds."[9] In other words, the theory of evolution survives despite the total lack of scientific evidence because the supporters of the theory need to believe evolution is true to escape the only logical alternative—that God both created the Universe and man, as well as the fact that we must face Him as our Creator at the end of our life to give an account of our response to His commands.

Why Cling to Evolution?

Why did so many scientists strongly support the theory of evolution when there is overwhelming evidence in every area of biological research that the theory was false? Despite the fact that the science textbooks and articles give the strong impression that the life-blood of science is the discovery of new truths, scientists are normal human beings that usually dislike having to abandon theories that they have embraced for most of their professional lives. The history of science reveals that new ideas, discoveries, and theories are usually resisted vigorously whenever they are first introduced. Virtually every new theory in science introduced during the last few centuries has initially been strongly resisted for many decades before the majority of scientists, intellectuals, and educators gradually accepted the evidence in support of the new teaching and embrace the new theory as true.

Despite the fact that scientific theories are based on facts and evidence, these facts cannot evaluate themselves to produce a coherent theory. All of the evidence that is discovered by scientists must be evaluated, interpreted, and coordinated with other data to finally fit into a theory that accounts for all of the known data. However, every scientist naturally brings his previous knowledge, training, experience, bias, and intellectual presuppositions with him when he evaluates any new evidence or theory. This is why a scientist can encounter a great deal of new evidence that contradicts his previously held theories and still find it quite difficult to admit that these theories are no longer true. These very natural human characteristics help explain why so many scientists have been so resistant to the fact that the theory of evolution is finally collapsing. However, thousands of scientists in multiple fields are slowly acknowledging the truth that their long-cherished theory is untenable.

Malcolm Muggeridge, a well-known British journal-
ist and philosopher, spoke at the Pascal Lectures, held
at the University of Waterloo in Ontario, Canada. Muggeridge dismissed the theory of evolution as one of the
great scientific frauds of the last century and a half. He
declared,

> I myself am convinced that the theory of evolu-
> tion, especially the extent to which it's been
> applied, will be one of the great jokes in the
> history books of the future. Posterity will marvel
> that so very flimsy and dubious an hypothesis
> could be accepted with the incredible credulity
> that it has.[10]

Atheism and Belief in God

An evolutionist, D. M. S. Watson, admitted:

> Evolution itself is accepted by zoologists, not
> because it has been observed to occur or can be
> proved by logical coherent evidence, but because
> the only alternative—special creation—is clearly
> *incredible*.[11]

God's verdict on the theory of evolution and on
the spiritual motives of those who embrace and teach
evolution while knowing that the evidence is entirely
lacking is revealed in the words of the Scriptures:

> For the wrath of God is revealed from heaven
> against all ungodliness and unrighteousness of
> men, who hold the truth in unrighteousness;
> because that which may be known of God is

manifest in them; for God hath shewed it unto them. For the invisible things of him from the creation of the world are clearly seen, being understood by the things that are made, even his eternal power and Godhead; so that they are without excuse: Because that, when they knew God, they glorified him not as God, neither were thankful; but became vain in their imaginations, and their foolish heart was darkened. Professing themselves to be wise, they became fools, and changed the glory of the incorruptible God into an image made like to corruptible man, and to birds, and fourfooted beasts, and creeping things. (Romans 1:18-23)

The Bible has only one statement regarding those who maintain there is no God despite the overwhelming evidence that exists to anyone who is willing to consider it. King David wrote,

The fool hath said in his heart, There is no God. They are corrupt, they have done abominable works, there is none that doeth good (Psalm 14:1).

The apostle Paul revealed that many people choose to reject the obvious evidence that our Universe and everything in it was purposely created by a divine Creator because they want to escape their responsibility to God. The truth is that all of creation proclaims the existence, the design, and the glory of a Creator. The psalmist David proclaimed the fact that the awesome beauty, vastness, and obvious design revealed the glory of the Creator to every man and woman.

The heavens declare the glory of God; and the firmament sheweth his handywork. Day unto day uttereth speech, and night unto night sheweth knowledge. There is no speech nor language, where their voice is not heard. Their line is gone out through all the earth, and their words to the end of the world. In them hath he set a tabernacle for the sun (Psalm 19:1-4).

There are two kinds of atheists: the ordinary atheist and the ornery kind. The ordinary atheist says, "I believe there is no God while I acknowledge that it is possible that you might have encountered evidence that convinces you that God exists." On the other hand the ornery atheist says, "There is no God, and you can't possibly know that there is a God either."

When we explain to an atheist that it is impossible that the Universe came into existence without a First Cause—namely, God—they often reply, "But who created God?" To this we answer, "God is a supernatural being existing outside the limitations of time and space in our Universe. Obviously, nothing that exists within our Universe of time and space could possibly create that Universe."

To our claim that "nothing comes from nothing," an atheist often replies that we claim God comes from nothing. However, this is not true. The Bible does not claim that God came from nothing. The Word of God declares that God has always existed, that He is an eternally existing being, without beginning or end. King David proclaimed the eternal nature of God: "Before the mountains were brought forth, or ever thou hadst formed the Earth and the world, even from everlasting to everlasting, thou art God" (Psalm 90:2).

The remarkable scientific discoveries during the last hundred years have proven that our Universe had a definite beginning at the moment of Creation and therefore, time, space, energy, and matter all began at some definite point in the distant past as the Bible declared: "In the beginning god created the heavens and the Earth" (Genesis 1:1). Since time itself began at Creation, we know that time cannot be infinite. Therefore, we can logically conclude that our Universe, which exists in time, must have been created by God, who exists outside of the limitations of time and space.

Many Scientists Support God's Creation

The incredible scientific discoveries in the last few decades have rocked the atheistic citadel of scientific opinion. Today, a growing number of scientists in fields as diverse as biology, genetics, paleontology, geology, and astronomy have confronted the implications of their own discoveries that totally contradict, not only the theory of evolution, but the very idea that the Universe we live in could ever have come into existence and developed the biological diversity we now witness everywhere unless it was designed by a supernatural intelligent Being following an intelligent design that staggers the mind.

As illustrated in this book, there is compelling evidence that is now accepted by the majority of living scientists that the Universe has not existed forever, despite that fact that the concept of a static Universe was almost universally taught and accepted during the first half of the twentieth century, until Dr. Edwin Hubble's discoveries illustrated the expanding Universe. Dr. Henry Margenau is Professor of Physics and Natural Philosophy, Yale University, and former president of the American Association for the Philosophy of Science. He acknowledged the compelling new scientific evidence that pointed toward the creation of the Universe from nothing.

> It is absolutely unreasonable to reject the notion of a Creator by appealing to science. Science has definitely shown the non-contradiction of Creation out of nothing."[12]

In other words, Margenau acknowledged that scientific evidence now supported the concept of instantaneous Creation out of nothing, as the Scriptures had proclaimed for thousands of years. Professor Margenau stated:

> Theories like the Big Bang, black holes, quantum theory, relativity, and the Anthropic Principle have introduced science to a world of awe and mystery that is not far removed from the ultimate mystery that drives the religious impulse. . . . What, then, is the answer to the question concerning the origin of the innumerable laws of nature? I know only one answer that is adequate to their universal validity: they were created by God.[13]

Professor Soren Lovtrup, an embryologist, wrote a book entitled *Darwinism: The Refutation of a Myth*, in which he totally repudiated the theory of evolution. Lovtrup wrote,

> I believe that one day the Darwinian myth will be ranked the greatest deceit in the history of science.[14]

The British astronomer Sir Fred Hoyle acknowledged that the evidence in favor of a purposeful Designer of this Universe is now overwhelming. The precision with which these scientific constants of physics and astronomy must fall within an exact criteria to permit life to exist is so overwhelming that many previously atheistic scientists were forced to the reluctant conclusion that the only possible logical conclusion is that our Universe was designed according to some precise plan that can only be described as "supernatural." After carefully considering the remarkable number of vital scientific factors governing the nature of our Universe that are now demonstrated to be precisely within exact parameters that will allow the existence of our both our Universe and human existence on Earth, Dr. Hoyle wrote:

> A common sense interpretation of the facts suggests that a superintellect has monkeyed with physics, as well as with chemistry and biology, and that there are no blind forces worth speaking about in nature. The numbers one calculates from the facts seem to me so overwhelming as to put this conclusion almost beyond question.[15]

Hoyle and Chandra Wickramasinghe wrote about

the growing evidence that points scientists toward a highly intelligent and purposeful Designer.

> Once we see, however, that the probability of life originating at random is so utterly minuscule as to make the random concept absurd, it becomes sensible to think that the favourable properties of physics on which life depends are in every respect deliberate. . . . It is therefore almost inevitable that our own measure of intelligence must reflect in a valid way the higher intelligences to our left, even to the extreme idealized limit of God.[16]

The astronomer George Greenstein wrote, in his 1988 book *The Symbiotic Universe*, that new scientific discoveries were providing compelling evidence that our Universe could not possibly have come into existence by chance alone.

> As we survey all the evidence, the thought insistently arises that some supernatural agency—or, rather, Agency—must be involved. Is it possible that suddenly, without intending to, we have stumbled upon scientific proof of the existence of a Supreme Being? Was it God who stepped in and so providentially crafted the cosmos for our benefit?[17]

Dr. Vera Kistiakowsky, a physicist from MIT, wrote,

> The exquisite order displayed by our scientific understanding of the physical world calls for the divine.[18]

Dr. Arthur L. Schawlow, professor of physics at

Stanford University and winner of the 1981 Nobel Prize for physics, wrote about the tremendous implications of recent astronomical discoveries and what they suggested about the nature of the Universe and its beginning. Professor Schawlow wrote,

> It seems to me that when confronted with the marvels of life and the Universe, one must ask why and not just how. The only possible answers are religious. . . . I find a need for God in the Universe and in my own life.[19]

An example of the acceptance of a Creator by leading scientists is Professor Richard Ferriman, the winner of the 1965 Nobel Prize in physics, who declared:

> Many scientists do believe in both science and God, the God of revelation, in a perfectly consistent way.[20]

As early as the 1980s, even the very secular-minded editors of *TIME* magazine were forced to acknowledge that a quiet but profound intellectual earthquake was occurring in the academic and scientific communities. After decades of academic and scientific rejection of the concept of Creation and an intelligent Designer of the Universe, the atheistic scientists were startled to discover that they were finding compelling evidence of a superintelligent design in the arrangement of the atoms, the Universe, the genetic DNA code, as well as the startlingly intricate and complex arrangement of every single biological system. In a significant article by *TIME* magazine in April 7, 1980, the writer declared:

In a quiet revolution in thought and argument that hardly anyone would have foreseen only two decades ago, God is making a comeback. Most intriguingly this is happening . . . in the crisp intellectual circles of academic philosophers.[21]

Dr. Richard Dawkins, an evolutionary professor at the Department of Zoology at Oxford University, has written about the evidence that points to the intelligent design throughout the Universe.

The more statistically improbable a thing is, the less can we believe that it just happened by blind chance. Superficially the obvious alternative to chance is an intelligent Designer.[22]

However, despite this telling admission, Dawkins still embraces the theory of evolution.

Professor Freeman Dyson, a physicist from Princeton University, acknowledged the revolution in the thinking of many scientists who were forced to confront the implications of the remarkable evidence for intelligent design they found in their own particular field of study. Dr. Dyson wrote,

The more I examine the Universe and the details of its architecture, the more evidence I find that the Universe in some sense must have known we were coming.[23]

In a discussion on the revolutionary changes now taking place in the world of science as a result of the recent discoveries about the nature of the Universe, the atom, and the discovery of DNA, Dr. Stephen Hawking wrote about the fact that these discoveries point to an obvious purposeful design.

> Then we shall . . . be able to take part in the discussion of the question of why it is that we and the Universe exist. If we find the answer to that, it would be the ultimate triumph of human reason—for then we would know the mind of God.[24]

A poll that questioned the religious behavior of 3,300 scientists was conducted for the professional society, Sigma Zi, and published under the title, "Scientists Are Anchored in the U.S. Mainstream." Remarkably, the poll discovered that 43 percent of Ph.D. scientists attend church on Sundays regularly. Intriguingly, that virtually parallels the rest of the citizens of the United States, where polls reveal that 44 percent attend church regularly.[25]

An American theoretical physicist, Professor James Trefil, wrote about the profound implications arising from the discoveries by scientists that point to the evidence that our Universe and humanity itself was purposely created. Dr. Trefil wrote,

> If I were a religious man, I would say that everything we have learned about life in the past twenty years shows that we are unique, and therefore special in God's sight. Instead I shall say that what we have learned shows that it matters a great deal what happens to us.[26]

Many of the leading scientists who lived in past centuries found no contradiction between their discoveries in science and their acceptance of the authority of Scripture regarding God's creation of the Universe. As an example, Johannes Kepler, who developed physical astronomy and the laws of planetary motion, believed strongly in God's Creation.

> I believe only and alone in the service of Jesus Christ. In him is all refuge and solace. When Kepler was asked his purpose in pursuing science, he responded that he wanted to complete scientific research to obtain a sample test of the delight of the Divine Creator in his work and to partake of his joy.[27]

Blaise Pascal, who died in 1662 in Paris, was a brilliant mathematician, scientist, and the inventor of a mechanical calculator that was three centuries ahead of its time. Pascal wrote,

> God makes people conscious of their inward wretchedness, which the Bible calls 'sin' and his infinite mercy. Unites himself to their inmost soul, fills it with humility and joy, with confidence and love, renders them incapable of any other end than Himself. Jesus Christ is the end of all and the center to which all tends.

As one of the most brilliant mathematicians of his day, Pascal invented the mathematical theory of probability. He also wrote,

> At the center of every human being is a God-shaped vacuum, which can only be filled by Jesus Christ.[28]

Robert Boyle developed the science of chemistry and gas dynamics. Boyle wrote a book entitled *The Wisdom of God Manifested in the Works of Creation* that affirmed his firm belief in the Word of God and the truth of God's creation.

Sir Isaac Newton is considered to be one of the greatest scientists in history. He was a brilliant mathematician, a scientist, and the founder of classical physics. When he contemplated the precision and supreme order displayed in the solar system and the heavens, Newton wrote:

This most beautiful system of the Sun, planets and comets could only proceed from the counsel and dominion of an intelligent and powerful Being.[29]

Sir Michael Faraday, the inventor of the electric generator, developed the science of electromagnetism. He was a strong Christian and, as he was dying, declared to a friend his unshakable faith in God:

Speculations, man, I have none. I have certainties. I thank God that I don't rest my dying head upon speculations for 'I know whom I have believed and am persuaded that he is able to keep that which I've committed unto him against that day.'[30]

Notes

1. B. G. Ranganathan, *Origins?* (Carlisle: The Banner of Truth Trust, 1988): 22.
2. G. A. Rerkut, *Implications of Evolution* (London: Pergamon Press, 1960): 150.
3. Internet web site: http://www.inplainsite.org/html/evolution.html
4. B. G. Ranganathan, *Origins?* (Carlisle, PA: The Banner of Truth Trust, 1988): 22.
5. Philip Johnson, *Darwin on Trial* (Washington, D.C.: Regnery Gateway, 1991): 59.
6. Philip Johnson, *Darwin on Trial* (Washington, D.C.: Regnery Gateway, 1991): 82.
7. Larry Hatfield, "Educators Against Darwin," *Science Digest Special* (Winter 1979), pp. 94–96.
8. W. R. Bird, The Origin of Species Revisited, Thomas Nelson Co., Nashville, 1991, p. 325.
9. Gershon Robinson and Mordechai Steinman, *The Obvious Proof* (New York: CIS Publishers, 1993) p. 87.
10. Malcolm Muggeridge, Pascal Lectures, University of Waterloo Research, *The Advocate*, March 8, 1984, p. 17.
11. D. M. S. Watson, "Adaptation," *Nature*, Vol. 123 [*sic* Vol. 124] (1929), p. 233.
12. Internet site: http://www.unnu.com/unnu/archive/etexts/qutationsonevolution.htm
13. Internet site: http://www.unnu.com/unnu/archive/etexts/qutationsonevolution.htm
14. Soren Lovtrup, *Darwinism: The Refutation of a Myth*. New York: Croom Helm, 1987, p. 422.

15. Sir Fred Hoyle, 1982. The Universe: Past and Present Reflections. *Annual Review of Astronomy and Astrophysics*: 20:16.
16. Sir Fred Hoyle and Chandra Wickramasinghe, "Convergence to God" Evolution from Space, London: J. M. Dent & Sons Ltd, 1981, p. 141 & 144.
17. G. Greenstein, 1988. *The Symbiotic Universe*. New York: William Morrow, p. 27.
18. H. Margenau and R. A. Varghese, eds. *Cosmos, Bios, Theos: Scientists Reflect on Science, God, and the Origins of the Universe, Life, and Homo Sapiens* (La Salle, IL, Open Court Pub. Co., 1992).
19. H. Margenau and R. A. Varghese, eds. Cosmos, Bios, Theos: *Scientists Reflect on Science, God, and the Origins of the Universe, Life, and Homo Sapiens* (Open Court Pub. Co., La Salle, IL, 1992.
20. Internet sit:http://www.inplainsite.org/html/a_scientist_and_a_christian.html
21. *Time*, April 7, 1980.
22. Richard Dawkins, "The necessity of Darwinism." *New Scientist*, vol. 94, 15 April 1982, p. 130.
23. Freeman Dyson, *Disturbing the Universe* (New York: Harper & row, 1979), p. 250.
24. Stephen Hawking, 1988. *A Brief History of Time*. New York: Bantam Books, p. 175.
25. Internet site: http://www.inplainsite.org/html/a_scientist_and_a_christian.html
26. Robert T. Rood and James S. Trefil, *Are We Alone? The Possibility of Extraterrestrial Civilizations* (New York: Charles Scribner's Sons, 1981), p. 247. Cited by Heeren, p. 220.

27. Ann Lamont, *21 Great Scientists Who Believed the Bible*, Answers in Genesis, Australia, 1995.
28. Internet site: http://www.ucolick.org/~ted/_christians.html
29. Isaac Newton, *Observations on the prophecy of Daniel and the Revelation of Saint John (1687)*.
30. Internet site: http://www.patlyons.com/m3325/chapters/Schaefer.htm

8

The Scientific Validity of the Bible

> We will not hide them from their children, shewing to the generation to come the praises of the Lord, and his strength, and his wonderful works that he hath done (Psalm 78:4).

> That I may publish with the voice of thanksgiving, and tell of all thy wondrous works (Psalm 26:7).

Many people are unaware of the fact that the Bible, although written thousands of years ago, contains numerous scientifically accurate statements that are impossible to explain apart from the Scripture's own claim that they are supernaturally inspired by God.

While the Bible is not a scientific textbook, whenever the Scriptures do include statements about scientific matters, these statements are stunning in their accuracy. Biblical statements reveal knowledge of science that is thousands of years ahead of what was known to the world when the writers penned the words of the Holy Scriptures. Consider God's "wondrous works" as displayed in the wonders of Creation in nature together with the advanced level of scientific knowledge present in the pages of the Bible as illustrated in this chapter. Some of this research appeared in my 1996 book, *The Signature of God*, but these facts are so related to the theme of this book on God's creation that they need to be included with additional new research in this chapter.

How could the writers of the Scriptures possibly know these scientific facts? The only logical conclusion is that God supernaturally inspired the human authors of the Scriptures to record these accurate scientific statements.

Throughout the Word of God, we read statements that can only now be tested as to their accuracy due to the tremendous advances in scientific knowledge in the last few decades. For example, the book of Genesis describes the supernatural creation of man in these words, "And the Lord God formed man of the dust of the ground, and breathed into his nostrils the breath of life; and man became a living soul" (Genesis 2:7). Scientists used to ridicule the apparent simplicity of the scriptural account that God used "the dust of the ground" to construct the incredibly complex proteins, molecules, and sixty trillion cells that make up a human being.

However, scientists were recently startled to

discover that the clay and Earth found in the "dust of the ground" do contain every single element found in the human body. A *Reader's Digest* article in November 1982 described this fascinating discovery by the researchers at NASA's Ames Research Center in California that confirmed the Bible's account that every single element found in the human body exists within the soil. The scientists concluded,

> We are just beginning to learn. The biblical scenario for the creation of life turns out to be not far off the mark.[1]

Science Confirms the Creation of the Universe

The book of Genesis begins with the words, "God created the heaven and the Earth" (Genesis 1:1). Until 1950, most scientists believed in some variation of the "steady state" theory, which suggested that the Universe had always existed as we observe it today. This theory was in total contradiction to the Word of God, which, as recorded in its opening pages, affirms that God created the entire Universe at a definite point in time in the distant past. New discoveries in the fields of astronomy and astrophysics since the 1930s forced the vast majority of the scientific world to change their theory to believe that the evidence now pointed to the definite beginning or creation of the Universe from one point or singularity. Today, most scientists accept that the whole Universe came into existence at a particular point in time, when an incredibly dense mass of matter rapidly expanded at a staggering speed, forming all of the stars, galaxies, and planets we witness today. The theory is supported by the observations from astronomy that all stars and galaxies appear to be moving away from each other at a tremendous speed.

However, in opposition to the theory of an aimless explosion as suggested in the so-called "Big Bang" theory, the Bible affirms that God, with absolute purpose and supernatural intelligence, created everything in the Universe to be inhabited by humans. The evidence from nature and the extraordinary scientific discoveries regarding the atom and DNA illustrated in this book reveal the meticulous intelligent design as well as the supernatural purpose and power of God in that initial moment of creation when "God created the heaven and the Earth."

Dr. P. Dirac, a Nobel Prize-winner from Cambridge University, wrote: "It seems certain that there was a definite time of creation." Until quite recently, the word *creation* was never written or spoken by scientists with approval. An article entitled "Creation of the Universe from Nothing," by Dr. A. Vilenkin, appeared in the 1982 issue of *Physical Letters*, an international journal of physics. While some scientists claim the creation of the Universe is "outside the scope of presently-known laws of physics," the overwhelming new evidence supports the biblical position that the Universe was definitely created at some point in time.[2]

The Bible Reveals the Vastness of Outer Space

The Scriptures record that God challenged Abraham to count the stars to demonstrate the awesome number of stars that He had created by His supernatural power. "Then he brought him forth abroad and said, Look now toward heaven, and tell the stars, if thou be able to number them: and he said unto him, So shall thy seed be" (Genesis 15:5). The unaided human eye can see and count approximately 6,000 stars. With a pair of binoculars or an inexpensive telescope, you can see almost 3,300 stars. In the last few years, modern telescopes have determined that there are over two hundred million stars in our own Milky Way galaxy alone.

Astronomers believed that our galaxy formed the entire Universe until new telescopes, developed around 1915, revealed the vast reaches of deep space. In 1925, the now-famous astronomer Professor Edwin Hubble used the new one-hundred-inch mirror telescope on Mount Wilson in southern California, the largest in the world at that time, to view whole new galaxies of stars containing millions of new stars that were more than six million trillion miles away from Earth. Hubble proved that the Universe contained at least as many galaxies outside our Milky Way as there were stars inside our home galaxy. During the last century, powerful telescopes revealed that the known Universe contains over ten billion galaxies such as our Milky Way.

After making massive improvements to the accuracy of the space mirror telescope that is now floating in Earth orbit approximately 300 miles above the planet's surface, scientists recently focused the Hubble Telescope on a tiny point in space as small a grain of sand held at arm's length from your eye. Astronomers intensely examined this very small point in space that revealed fifteen hundred new galaxies, each the size of our Milky

Way. They were astonished to discover that the Universe is more than five times larger than previously believed. They now know that the known Universe contains more than fifty billion galaxies, with each galaxy containing hundreds of millions of stars. The mind of man can scarcely conceive of such a vast Universe in which fifty billion galaxies, each containing hundreds of millions of stars, extend out from our solar system for untold trillions of miles in every direction. However, the question arises: How could Moses, the human author of Genesis writing 3500 years ago, possibly know that the staggering number of stars in the heavens was far beyond the ability of a man living in the ancient Middle East to even begin to count? *(See picture section, figure 18.)*

To obtain a sense of the true vastness of our Universe, try this exercise. Take a piece of paper and draw two circles with a small circle representing our Sun at the top of the page. Using the scale of one inch to represent ten million miles, we draw a much smaller circle nine inches lower at the bottom of the page to represent our Earth. Now let's draw another small circle to represent our nearest neighboring star, Alpha Centauri. You would need to draw the small circle representing the star Alpha Centauri over forty miles away from your piece of paper to correctly represent the vast distance between our Earth and our closest neighboring star. Light travels through space at an amazing speed of 186,280 miles every second, or six trillion miles every year. A ray of light leaving Alpha Centauri would take four years to reach our planet as it crosses an astonishing twenty-four trillion miles of outer space.

The psalmist David wrote,

By the word of the Lord the heavens were made, and all the host of them by the breath of His mouth. . . . For he spake, and it was done; he commanded, and it stood fast (Psalm 33:6, 9).

Despite all of the billions spent on astronomy, scientists have failed to come up with a credible theory to account for the existence of either the Universe or even our own planet. In 1980, astronomer Professor Herman Bondi announced the total failure of modern science to yet account for the existence of the Universe:

As an erstwhile cosmologist, I speak with feeling of the fact that theories of the origin of the Universe have been disproved by present day empirical evidence as have various theories of the origin of the solar system.[3]

Another important astronomer, Sir Harold Jeffreys, wrote,

To sum up, I think that all suggested accounts of the origin of the solar system are subject to serious objections. The conclusion in the present state of the subject would be that the system cannot exist.[4]

In other words, Professor Jeffreys admitted that none of the current theories can account for the Universe as it exists. The real answer is found in the words in Genesis as recorded by Moses, "In the beginning God created the heaven and the Earth" (Genesis 1:1).

Water Found in Deep Space

Another remarkable scientific fact recorded in the Scriptures is found in the book of Genesis. The Bible declares that God separated the waters below (in the Earth) from the waters that were above (in the heavens):

> And God said, Let there be a firmament in the midst of the waters, and let it divide the waters from the waters. And God made the firmament, and divided the waters which were under the firmament from the waters which were above the firmament: and it was so (Genesis 1:6-7).

This 3,500-hundred-year-old biblical statement declared that God created a large amount of water that He placed in the heavens, or in deep space.

Is there any scientific evidence that supports this intriguing ancient biblical statement? The existence of water in space seemed improbable, if not impossible, to scientists until quite recently. However, new astronomical discoveries have revealed that massive amounts of water exist in outer space, exactly as the Bible originally claimed. Naturally, because of the extremely cold temperature found in space, these waters are frozen into ice. Recently, U.S. satellites discovered enormous quantities of water frozen within the northern and southern ice caps of Mars, as well as in the extraordinarily beautiful rings of ice and dust circling the planet Saturn. In addition, astronomers discovered that the comets traveling through our solar system are composed of massive amounts of ice and rock.

A meteor composed of a huge block of ice and rock

from space collided with the Earth at the beginning of the last century in a remote part of Siberia in northern Russia:

> In the morning of 30 June 1908, a fantastic explosion occurred in central Siberia. . . . Witnesses described an enormous meteoric bolide visible in the sky for a few seconds. Other witnesses from a distance of 60 kilometers (36 miles) from the point of impact were knocked over. . . . Seismic shocks were registered over the whole world . . . this event was due to the collision with the Earth of a block of ice weighing 30,000 tons which . . . released energy equivalent to that of a thermonuclear bomb of 12 megatons.[5]

Researchers believe that this Siberian explosion was caused by a very small fragment of the comet Encke that broke away during its passage through our solar system.

The latest scientific research revealed that tremendous amounts of ice also exist at the outer edge of our solar system. Astronomers now believe that there is a vast region of space at the edge of our solar system that holds perhaps a trillion large comets composed of ice and rock. Each large comet is believed to contain up to one trillion tons of ice. The vast amount of water in the Earth's oceans is a small fraction of the quantities of water that exist in the "firmament above," as reported in the Genesis passage. Another passage in Job also refers to the ice and frost found in the heavens:

> Hath the rain a father? or who hath begotten the

drops of dew? Out of whose womb came the ice? and the hoary frost of heaven, who hath gendered it? The waters are hid as with a stone, and the face of the deep is frozen. Canst thou bind the sweet influences of Pleiades, or loose the bands of Orion? (Job 38:28-31).

How could someone like Job, living, during ancient times, in the hot climate of what is now Saudi Arabia, have known about frozen ice caps in the far north and south of our planet?

The First Law of Thermodynamics: Conservation of Energy

After many experiments, scientists discovered two fundamental laws of the science of thermodynamics that describe the basic nature of our Universe. These laws are absolute—science has never found an exception. The first law is known as the Law of Conservation of Energy, which declares that "energy can be neither created nor destroyed." The famous science writer Isaac Asimov defined this Law of Conservation of Energy as follows:

> Energy can be transferred from one place to another, or transformed from one form to another, but it can be neither created nor destroyed.[6]

In other words, this law states that the total amount of energy that exists throughout our Universe remains constant and can never change. For example, when they explode a nuclear device, the uranium and plutonium within the warhead are not annihilated. The matter does not cease to exist. The potential energy within the nuclear elements is released as a staggering amount of both heat and light energy. Every experiment has confirmed this Law of Conservation of Energy as the most basic fundamental understanding of the way the Universe works. There are no known exceptions to this law. This law describes the present state of the Universe after its initial creation by God.

The law of the Conservation of Energy was scientifically discovered and proven during the last century. However, the Word of God recorded this principle thousands of years ago. Moses wrote in Genesis:

> And on the seventh day *God ended his work which he had made;* and he rested on the seventh day from all his work which he had made. And God blessed the seventh day, and sanctified it: because that in it *he had rested from all his work which God created and made"* (Genesis 2:2-3, emphasis added).

In other words, after God created man on the sixth day of Creation week, His creative work was now finished and complete. This accounts for the truth of the First Law of Conservation of Energy. In addition, the Scriptures reveal why matter and energy cannot *now* be either totally destroyed or annihilated because God's supernatural Creation is complete. The Scriptures declare that Jesus Christ, who created all things, is *now*, since Creation, "upholding all things by the word of his power" (Hebrews 1:3). In another Scriptural passage, the writer of the book of Hebrews declared that Jesus, the Creator of the Universe, had finished His acts of creation (Hebrews 4:10).

The Second Law of Thermodynamics:
Entropy

The second fundamental law of science is known as the Second Law of Thermodynamics: Entropy. This law describes the fact that all systems and elements in our Universe tend to disintegrate (fall to a lower order of available energy or organization). Another way of expressing the universal fact of entropy is to note that, over time, all things, whether a house or a sword, will tend to disintegrate to dust or rust, obviously a lower order of organization than the original new house or polished sword. Throughout history, humanity has observed that everything, from a human body to a house, begins to decay from the moment of maximum amount of order or organized information at the beginning until, years later, the object ceases to function and falls apart. This universal principle of entropy proves that it is absolutely impossible for the theory of evolution to be true. Evolution declares that the most simple biological systems become increasingly more organized and complicated through the process of accidental chance mutations and natural selection. However, common-sense observations and scientific observations have proven that all systems and all elements on Earth tend to disintegrate over time, dissipating energy as they go. The Second Law of Thermodynamics, entropy, proves that the theory of evolution is scientifically untenable.

The Law of Conservation of Energy proves that the Universe could never have created itself without an outside supernatural being. The "heavens and the Earth" must have been created by a supernatural force outside the Universe. The law of entropy shows that the whole Universe is running down as it decays to a lower order of available energy. The book of Romans in the New Testament alludes to this law of entropy in the Apostle Paul's statement:

> For we know that the whole creation groaneth and travaileth in pain together until now (Romans 8:22).

The scientific reality of entropy confirms that the Universe must have been created at some point in the past and has been running down like a wound-up clock ever since that initial moment of Creation. If we find a watch that is running down, we know that originally someone must have purposely created it and someone also wound it up. Since the Universe is scientifically demonstrated to be "running down" according to the law of entropy, the logical inference is that the Universe must have been created by an outside supernatural source at some point in the distant past.

The Earth Is a Sphere

Atheistic critics of the Scriptures often attacked Christianity by falsely claiming that the Bible actually declares that "the Earth is flat." They have quoted two Scriptural passages that simply express normal biblical colloquial expressions about the Earth including the phrases, "the four corners of the Earth," which appear in both Isaiah 11:12 and Revelation 7:1. For example, the prophet Isaiah wrote, "And he shall set up an ensign for the nations, and shall assemble the outcasts of Israel, and gather together the dispersed of Judah from *the four corners of the Earth."* This common expression *"four corners of the Earth"* also appears in the text of the New Testament in the book of Revelation, where the prophet John wrote,

> And after these things I saw four angels standing on the *four corners of the Earth*, holding the four winds of the Earth, that the wind should not blow on the Earth, nor on the sea, nor on any tree (Revelation 7:1).

The expression was common in ancient times and is still used by many educated individuals in a coloquial manner without ever intending to express the ridiculous view that critics foolishly suggest implies that the speaker actually intended to express his belief in a "flat Earth". *(See picture section, figure 15.)*

Some liberal critics declared that the biblical writers actually believed in a "flat Earth." However, this phrase "the four corners of the Earth" was simply a colloquial expression commonly used in both the ancient and modern world. The expression is still commonly used by educated individuals to indicate either the whole of the planet Earth or the four extremities of the globe as viewed on a map from a central position.

The truth is that God actually inspired the ancient prophet Isaiah to reveal that our planet was a globe. The fact that our Earth is a sphere was scientific knowledge that was far in advance of what the men living 2500 years ago actually knew. However, the prophet Isaiah wrote about God's creation of the sphere of the Earth as follows:

It is he that sitteth upon *the circle of the Earth*, and the inhabitants thereof are as grasshoppers; that stretcheth out the heavens as a curtain, and spreadeth them out as a tent to dwell in (Isaiah 40:22).

The expression "the circle of the Earth" clearly refers to the Earth as a sphere or globe.

Another interesting scientific statement found in the ancient pages of the New Testament is a passage that confirms the reality of the Earth as a spherical globe. The Gospel writer Luke documented Jesus' words of his future second coming, saying it will occur in the daytime: "Even thus shall it be in the day when the Son of man is revealed" (Luke 17:30). However, several verses later, Jesus again described the same event by declaring that Christ will come in the night: "I tell you, in that night there shall be two men in one bed; the one shall be taken, and the other shall be left" (Luke 17:34). To the natural mind of a reader in the first century, Jesus' words must have sounded like a logical contradiction.

How could a single future event, the coming of the Messiah, occur simultaneously "in the day" and "in the night"? Jesus' statement must have seemed impossible. It appeared to be a logical contradiction throughout the many centuries until scientists finally proved that we live on a globe. However, since the discovery that we live on a spherical globe, we now understand that, on whatever day in the future that Christ returns, it will obviously be a daytime event for those living on one side of the Earth while the same awesome Second Coming event will occur during the night for those living on the other side of the planet.

The Circuit of the Sun

King David wrote a wonderful song of praise to God in recognition of His awesome glory displayed in the heavens that the king could witness with his own eyes from the roof of his palace in Jerusalem:

> Their line is gone out through all the Earth, and their words to the end of the world. In them hath he set a tabernacle for the Sun, which is as a bridegroom coming out of his chamber, and rejoiceth as a strong man to run a race. His going forth is from the end of the heaven, and his circuit unto the ends of it: and there is nothing hid from the heat thereof (Psalm 19:4-6).

Many Bible critics have denounced this statement of David's as false, claiming the Bible had declared that the Sun moved in an orbit around the Earth. However, the Bible never made that false claim. Instead, the Scriptures correctly declare that the Sun moved in "his circuit unto the ends of [the heavens]."

The Scripture's ancient statement about the Sun's movement through the heavens turns out to actually be scientifically true! Recent discoveries by astronomers working with the newly-improved Hubble telescope have confirmed the accuracy of the Scriptural account as they proved that the Sun is actually moving through space in a circuit covering an enormous orbit that will take over two hundred and sixty million years. But how could King David have possibly known this scientific fact three thousand years ago unless God inspired him to record these statements?

The Earth and Empty Space

The book of Job tells us, "He stretcheth out the north over the empty place, and hangeth the Earth upon nothing" (Job 26:7). This was a very advanced and accurate scientific statement. The ancient pagans who lived at the time of Job believed that the Earth was balanced on the back of an elephant that rested on the back of a turtle. Other pagans believed that the mythical hero Atlas carried the Earth on his shoulders. However, four thousand years ago, Job was inspired by God to correctly declare that God "hangeth the Earth upon nothing." Only a century ago scientists believed that the Earth and stars were supported by some kind of ether.

A "Hole in Space" Mentioned in the Bible

An interesting discovery by astronomers recently revealed that the area to the north of the axis of our Earth toward the polar star is almost empty of stars, as compared with all other directions. There are far more distant stars in every other direction from our Earth than in the area to the far north of our planet. As Job reported, "He stretcheth out the north over the empty place" (Job 26:7). Mitchell Waldrop wrote the following statement in an article in *Science* magazine.

The recently announced 'hole in space,' a 300

million-light-year gap in the distribution of galaxies, has taken cosmologists by surprise. . . . But three very deep core samples in the Northern Hemisphere, lying in the general direction of the constellation Bootes, showed striking gaps in the red shift distribution.[7]

This relative emptiness of stars in the direction to the north of our solar system is not visible to the naked eye. It is only as the result of very careful observation by telescopes that scientists have recently proven that the book of Job contained accurate information about astronomy that no one could have known apart from God's inspriration.

The Hydrological Weather Cycle

The Scriptures contain statements revealing advanced scientific knowledge about the hydrological cycle that governs the global climate and permits life to flourish. People living in past centuries did not have a clear understanding about the incredible complexity of the weather and climatic patterns that control the Earth's environment. However, the Old Testament books of Job, Ecclesiastes, Isaiah, and Jeremiah all describe details about the complexity of the weather system far beyond the knowledge of the people living at that time. The complete hydrological cycle governing evaporation, cloud formation, thunder, lightning, and rain is explained in surprising detail in the words of the Old Testament. For example, Ecclesiastes states, "If the clouds be full of rain, they empty themselves upon the Earth" (Ecclesiastes 11:3).

Throughout history, most people lived far from the coasts, and had very little awareness of the vast oceans that we now know covered over two-thirds of the planet's surface. They naturally assumed that the known evaporation of water from the surface of the lakes and rivers was primarily responsible for the clouds. However, the inspired book of Ecclesiastes confirms that most clouds are actually formed by evaporation from the oceans covering the majority of the Earth's surface:

> All the rivers run into the sea, yet the sea is not full; to the place from which the rivers come, there they return again (Ecclesiastes 1:7).

A recent study by the United States Department of Agriculture proved that most of the water that forms into the clouds worldwide comes from the evaporation of the waters found in the oceans that cover over 70 percent of the planet's surface. But how did the ancient writer of Ecclesiastes know these scientific facts three thousand years ago, when the vast extent of the oceans were not known?

The book of Job asked the question,

> Dost thou know the balancings of the clouds, the wondrous works of him which is perfect in knowledge? (Job 37:16).

When you consider the heavy weight of water compared to air, it is astonishing that enormous quantities of water are raised from the oceans and lakes every hour by evaporation and lifted thousands of feet into the air, where it remains suspended for long periods of time. Air rises upward as it cools, supporting the water vapor in the clouds until the drops become large and heavy enough to fall to Earth as rain. The answer is also found in Job:

> For he maketh small the drops of water: they pour down rain according to the vapour thereof: which the clouds do drop and distil upon man abundantly. Also can any understand the spreadings of the clouds, or the noise of his canopy? (Job 36:27-29).

This biblical passage reveals the complete hydrological cycle of evaporation, cloud formation, and precipitation.

The Complexity of Weather Patterns

Three millennia ago, King Solomon described the complex circular global wind patterns that determine the weather throughout the Earth.

> The wind goeth toward the south, and turneth about unto the north; it whirleth about continually, and the wind returneth again according to his circuits (Ecclesiastes 1:6).

How could Solomon have known that the planetary winds followed a circular pattern from south to north and south again?

The book of Job speaks of God controlling the weather:

For he looketh to the ends of the Earth, and seeth under the whole heaven; to make the weight for the winds; and he weigheth the waters by measure. When he made a decree for the rain and a way for the lightning of the thunder (Job 28:24-26).

Meteorologists have found that the relative weights of the wind and water greatly determine weather patterns. How could Job have known that the air and the wind patterns are governed by their actual weight?

Lightning and Thunder

The Bible also reveals a profound appreciation of the fact that there is a scientific connection between lightning, thunder, and the triggering of rainfall. Apparently, the slightest change in the electrical charge within a cloud is a key factor that causes microscopic water droplets in the clouds to join with other droplets until they are heavy enough to fall to Earth. In addition, we now know that a powerful electrical charge as high as 300 million volts in a cloud sends a leader stroke down, creating a path through the air to the ground. Only one-fiftieth of a second later, a second, more powerful return stroke travels back up to the cloud, following the path through the air opened by the leader stroke. The thunder occurs because the air within this channel or path has been vaporized by superheating it to 50,000 degrees by the lightning. The superheated air expands outward at supersonic speed, creating the noise of thunder. Job's description, "He made a decree for the rain and a way for the lightning of the thunder" (Job 28:26) is startling in its accuracy. No human could have known this in ancient times without the divine revelation of God.

The Paths of the Sea

King David, the writer of many of the Psalms, refers mysteriously to "the paths of the seas." He wrote,

> The fowl of the air, and the fish of the sea, and whatsoever passeth through the paths of the seas (Psalm 8:8).

In 1786, Benjamin Franklin published the information he gleaned from conversations with ocean-going captains—namely that huge currents, such as the Gulf Stream, ran like deep rivers far beneath the surface of the Atlantic Ocean. The massive Gulf Stream carries more than five thousand times as much water as the great Mississippi River. This awesome river current, that warms the climate of the U.K. and Western Europe, carries more than twenty-five times as much water as all the rivers on the planet combined. Scientists have discovered that the enormous Gulf Stream is only a small part of an enormous "gyre," a huge thirteen-thousand-mile-long, deep underwater current circling the Atlantic Ocean. They recently discovered that the Pacific Ocean has its own "Black Current" gyre as well.

CNN ran a news report in May 1996 of marine scientists' discovery of a massive river of water flowing north beneath the Pacific Ocean, parallel to the coast of the western United States. However, they also found that another huge current ran underneath the surface of the ocean but above the first huge current, except that this higher current flowed south at a very fast flow rate. The turbulence produced by these opposing currents passing each other at different depths in the Pacific produced massive underwater storms deep beneath the surface of the ocean. These currents not only warm the north of the planet, but they are also essential to refreshing the otherwise stagnant waters of the ocean and constitute an essential part of the life systems on the planet. How could King David, living in Israel and surrounding nations throughout his life, have known, thousands of years ago, that there were incredibly huge currents under the surface rivers that existed in the enormous depths of the boundless oceans?

The "Springs of the Sea"

In another passage, Job referred to deep springs of water at the bottom of the ocean.

> Hast thou entered into the springs of the sea? or hast thou walked in the search of the depth? (Job 38:16).

In this verse, the Bible refers to the existence of springs of water flowing in the depths of the sea. It is only in the last thirty years that underwater exploration of the ocean depths has revealed a remarkable phenomenon of numerous huge springs of fresh water pouring out of the ocean floor.

The many scientific statements found throughout the Bible are one of the greatest proofs of God's inspiration of the Scriptures. Significantly, there are no scientific errors or mistakes that have been discovered in the thousands of pages of inspired passages. These conclusive evidences provide overwhelming proof that God exists, and that He truly inspired the writers of Scripture to record His message to all of mankind. The fascinating scientific insights revealed in the pages of the Bible, from Genesis to Revelation, are God's authentic signature on the pages of the Scriptures, proving it is the genuine Word of God.

Notes

1. "How Life on Earth Began," *Reader's Digest*,
   November, 1982, p. 116.
2. A Vilenkin, Creation of Universes From Nothing,
   Physics Letters, Vol. 117B No. 1,2 (4 November 1982)
3. Herman Bondi, "Letters Section," *New Scientist*,
   August 21, 1980
4. Harold Jeffreys, *The Earth: Its Origin, History, and
   Physical Constitution* (1970), p. 359.
5. http://www.madladdesigns.co.uk/unexplained/
   enigmas/tunguska.htm
6. Isaac Asimov: "In the Game of Energy and
   Thermodynamics You Can't Break Even,"
   Smithsonian Institute Journal, June, 1970, p. 6.
7. Mitchell Waldrop, "Delving the Hole in Space,"
   Science Magazine, Nov. 27, 1981.

9

Meeting the Designer

In the final analysis, the new scientific evidence confirming the intelligent design of the Universe and life itself, together with the collapse of evolution, provides compelling reasons to believe that God inspired the Bible's account of Creation. These remarkable discoveries by scientists challenge every one of us to carefully consider the implications of the supernatural creation of the Universe.

The evidence presented in *Creation* shows that the Genesis account of God's creation of the "heaven and the Earth" is consistent with recent discoveries in astronomy, nuclear physics, and genetics. The remarkable scientific discoveries made during the last few decades strongly support the biblical position that our Universe and humanity itself were created by God with an intelligent purpose and plan. Therefore, each one of us must decide if we will personally accept or reject the implications of the fact that our Universe, and we ourselves, have been created by a supernatural Being to fulfill a divine purpose.

The only written instructions that we have received regarding this purpose and plan are found in the Bible. The Scriptures contain a remarkable and accurate description of the creation of the Universe, the Earth, and humanity. As this book demonstrates, the Bible also contains many extraordinary and accurate scientific statements that could not possibly have been known by the human authors thousands of years ago, when they wrote these texts. Therefore, we can logically conclude that God inspired the Bible.

Our personal response to the question about the purpose of the Universe and mankind will depend on our evaluation of the Scriptural account in Genesis and the scientific evidence supporting Creation that we have explored in this book. However, God never told us, "Believe in the Bible's account of Creation and you shall be saved." The demons and Satan know that the Scriptures are true, but this intellectual knowledge will not save them. Rather, it is significant that the Bible tells us: "Believe on the Lord Jesus Christ, and thou shall be saved, and thy house" (Acts 16:31). The clear message repeated throughout the Scriptures is that our personal relationship to God is what will determine our personal eternal destiny—heaven or hell.

The Scriptures repeatedly declare that Jesus Christ is God and that He is the Creation who purposely created the Universe and humanity.

For by him were all things created, that are in heaven, and that are in Earth, visible and invisible, whether they be thrones, or dominions, or principalities, or powers: all things were created by him, and for him: And he is before all things, and by him all things consist (Colossians 1:16-17).

The Nature of God

What is the nature of God, who created the Universe and humanity? For thousands of years, men have attempted in every culture and society to determine the nature of God. They have created God in their own image, in the image of the Sun, moon, stars, the Earth, and a hundred other objects. Regardless of his philosophical speculations about the divine intelligence that created our Universe, man will never be able to find the truth about God unless he is willing to accept God's own written revelation regarding His nature and His commands to humanity. The Bible, from Genesis to Revelation, reveals the nature of God as a loving, holy, powerful personality who is vitally interested in the lives and destiny of humans.

Years ago, philosophers assigned the term the First Cause to describe God as the intelligent supernatural Designer who created our Universe. Consider the necessary nature of the First Cause, God the Creator, and the nature of the Universe He created in light of the overwhelming evidence that we have explored in this book.

The First Cause of limitless Space must be infinite in extent.

The First Cause of endless Time must be eternal in duration.

The First Cause of unbounded Variety must be omnipresent in phenomena.

The First Cause of infinite Complexity must be omniscient in intelligence.

The First Cause of Consciousness must be personal.

The First Cause of Feeling must be emotional.

The First Cause of Will must be volitional.

The First Cause of Ethical values must be moral.

The First Cause of Religious values must be spiritual.

The First Cause of Righteousness must be holy.

The First Cause of Justice must be just.

The First Cause of Love must be loving.

The First Cause of Life must be alive.

This analysis reveals that the First Cause of all things, God the Creator, must be infinite, eternal, omnipresent, omniscient, personal, emotional, volitional, moral, spiritual, holy, just, loving, and alive. When we examine the nature of God as revealed through both Creation and the Scriptures, we discover that the Creator of the Universe is precisely as described above.

Our Response

The recent discoveries of scientists in astronomy, atomic physics, and genetics reveal that the extraordinary account of God's creation of heavens and the Earth as well as the creation of life itself occurred as recorded in the book of Genesis. The compelling evidence for intelligent design of our Universe as presented in this book provides convincing proof that God created everything, as the Bible declares. Our personal decision as to whether or not God truly created the cosmos is vital because this decision will affect every other area of our lives. If the Bible's claims about God's creation are true, then we are obviously accountable to our Creator God, who will ultimately judge each of us at the end of our life regarding our life and our response to our Creator.

In light of the overwhelming evidence presented in this book confirming that our Universe, our solar system, Earth, and life itself can only be the result of intelligent design, any fair-minded reader can see that only a supernatural, intelligent Designer could have produced our Universe. The evidence in this book also proves that the Bible contains accurate scientific information that could not have been known thousands of years ago unless God supernaturally inspired the human writers.

However, there are many people who will still reject the Bible's claim that God created the Universe and its claim that the Scriptures are the inspired Word of God. The problem facing those readers who still refuse to acknowledge the compelling scientific evidence for supernatural creation is not simply a problem of belief. Their problem is their refusal to accept the overwhelming evidence that challenges their long-held atheistic position of chance evolution. While such people can see the powerful evidence supporting the Bible's account of supernatural creation, they cannot bring themselves to accept the inevitable logical conclusion because they would then have to abandon their previously-held atheistic position to which they are emotionally and intellectually committed. In other words, their problem is not that they *cannot* believe the evidence before their eyes; the problem is that they *will not* believe the ample evidence pointing to the truth of the Bible's account of Creation, no matter how powerfully the scientific evidence points to this conclusion.

Many individuals who have rejected Creation and the Bible's account of God's intelligent design of our Universe have a huge personal investment in their openly-declared position of atheistic evolution. When they are faced with the evidence that points clearly to special creation, they are threatened by this evidence because it requires them to seriously re-think their position about God as Creator and their ultimate personal responsibility to Him. Many people have avoided thinking about God and eternity by hiding behind their denials of God's Creation. However, in light of the fascinating evidence provided in *CREATION*, we need to carefully consider the implications of the fact that science now points to our Universe being designed with purpose by a supernatural intelligence. If the Bible is truly the Word of God, then someday every one of us will stand before God at the end of our life to give an account for our response to Him.

The apostle Peter spoke about the absolute necessity of our personal faith in Jesus Christ: "Neither is there salvation in any other: for there is none other name under heaven given among men, whereby we must be saved" (Acts 4:12). This biblical declaration runs totally counter to the natural inclination of modern thinking that chooses to believe that all religions are equally true and that "all roads lead to Rome." Many in our modern society believe that if a person is truly sincere, that regardless of their beliefs, God will allow him to enter Heaven. However, the Word of God declares that sincerity is not enough. If you are sincere in your faith but have chosen to place your faith in a false religion, then you are sincerely wrong. The consequences of this rejection of God's only plan of salvation are eternal.

According to the Bible, there is only one way to reconcile ourselves as sinners to God. The true path to salvation according to the Bible is through personal repentance of our sins and placing our total faith in Christ's sacrificial death on the Cross. Every one of us has rebelled against God and His commands through our personal sins: "For all have sinned, and come short of the glory of God" (Romans 3:23). The Scriptures declare that our personal sinful rebellion has alienated each of us from the holiness of God and therefore prevents us from ever entering the holiness of heaven unless God forgives our sins. The Scriptures declare, "For the wages of sin is death; but the gift of God is eternal life through Jesus Christ our Lord" (Romans 6:23). The death of Jesus Christ on the Cross is the key to bringing us to a place of true spiritual peace in our heart. The death of our sinful rebellious nature when we identify with Christ's death is the key to finding true salvation and peace with God.

God cannot allow unrepentant sinners into heaven unless they repent of their sins. The sacred nature of heaven and the evil nature of sin make it absolutely impossible for God to forgive men's sins unless they freely and wholeheartedly repent and turn from their sinful rebellion. Only then can God forgive and transform us into sinners saved by the supernatural grace of Jesus Christ who cleanses us from our sinful rebellion against His laws. Although we can cleanse our bodies with water, the cleansing of our souls requires the supernatural application of the grace of Jesus Christ to motivate us to ask Him to forgive our sins.

The Gospel of John records the answer Jesus gave to Nicodemus, one of the religious leaders of Israel, who asked Him about personal salvation. Jesus told him that, "Ye must be born again" (John 3:7). Jesus explained to Nicodemus, "Whosoever believeth in him should not perish, but have eternal life. For God so loved the world, that he gave his only begotten Son, that whosoever believeth in him should not perish, but have everlasting life" (John 3:15-16). Every sinner stands condemned by God because of their sinful rebellion against His commandments as revealed in the Scriptures. Jesus said, "He that believeth on him is not condemned: but he that believeth not is condemned already, because he hath not believed in the name of the only begotten Son of God" (John 3:18).

Your decision to accept or reject Christ as your personal Savior is the most important decision you will ever make. It will cost you a great deal to live as a committed Christian today. Many people will challenge your new faith in the Bible and in Christ. The Lord Jesus Christ said to his disciples, "Follow me." Your decision and commitment to follow Christ will change your life forever. Your commitment to Christ will unleash His supernatural grace and power to transform your life into one of purpose, joy, and peace beyond anything you have ever experienced. While your commitment to follow Jesus Christ as your Lord and Savior will cost you a great deal, it will cost you everything if you are not a Christian at the final moment when you die. Jesus challenges us with these words, "For what shall it profit a man, if he shall gain the whole world, and lose his own soul?" (Mark 8:36).

If you are already a Christian, I challenge you to share the evidence in this book to witness to your friends about the truth of the Bible's account of Creation and your personal faith in Jesus Christ. The powerful new scientific evidence that our Universe was truly created by God and that the Bible is inspired by God will not, by itself, convince anyone to place their faith in Jesus Christ. However, this compelling evidence proving the truthfulness of the Bible's claims about Creation may remove the intellectual barriers that many people in modern society have raised against seriously considering the claims of Jesus Christ. Once they acknowledge the Scripture's authority, they can begin to consider whether or not they want to accept the Gospel's account of Jesus Christ's death and resurrection and His offer of salvation for any who will accept His forgiveness of our sins.

You have seen the evidence. The final decision is yours.

Selected Bibliography

Aviezer, Nathan. *In the Beginning*. Hoboken: KTAV
Publishing House, 1995.

Baugh, Carl E. *Why Do Men Believe Evolution Against
All Odds?*. Oklahoma City: Hearthstone Publishing,
1999.

Behe, Michael J. *Darwin's Black Box*. New York: The
Free Press, 1996.

Bowden, M. *The Rise of the Evolution Fraud*. San Diego:
Creation-Life Publishers, 1982.

Bowden, M. *Science vs Evolution*. Bromley: Sovereign
Publications, 1991.

Bowden, Malcolm. *Ape-Men*. Bromley: Sovereign
Publications, 1988.

Broom, Neil. *How Blind Is The Watchmaker?* Downers
Grove, Illinois. InterVarsity Press. 2001.

Brouwer, Sigmund. *The Unrandom Universe*. Eugene: Harvest House Publishers, 2002.

Brown, Dovid. *Mysteries of the Creation*. Southfield: Targum Press, Inc., 1997.

Collins, Gary R. *The Magnificent Mind*. Waco: Word Books Publisher, 1985.

Dembski, William A. *Intelligent Design*. Downers Grove, Illinois: InterVarsity Press, 1999.

Dembski, William A. *No Free Lunch*. Oxford: Rowman & Littlefield Publishers, Inc., 2002.

Dembski, William A., editor. *Mere Creation*. Downers Grove, Illinois: InterVarsity Press, 1998.

Dembski, William A and James M. Kushiner. *Signs of Intelligence*. Grand Rapids: Brazos Press, 2001.

Denton, Michael J. *Nature's Destiny*. New York: The Free Press, 1998.

Eastman, Mark and Chuck Missler. *The Creator Beyond Time and Space*. Costa Mesa: The Word For Today, 1996.

Gish, Duane T. *Creation Scientists Answer Their Critics*. El Cajon: Institute for Creation Research, 1993.

Gish, Duane T. *Evolution: The Fossils Still Say No!*. El Cajon: Institute for Creation Research, 1995.

Glynn, Patrick. *God The Evidence*. Rocklin: Prima Publishing, 1999.

Ham, Ken. *Why Won't They Listen?*. Greenforest: Master Books Inc., 2002.

Hawking, Stephen. *The Universe in a Nutshell*. New York: Bantam Books, 2001.

Heeren, Fred. *Show Me God*. Wheeling: Day Star Publications, 1997.

Huse, Scott M. *The Collapse of Evolution*. Grand Rapids: Baker Book House, 1990.

Katz, Avrohom. *Designer World*. Gateshead: GJBS, 1994.

Leslie, John. *Universes*. London: Routledge, 1996.

Levitt, I. M. *Beyond the Known Universe*. New York: The Viking Press, Inc., 1974.

Lubenow, Marvin L. *Bones of Contention*. Grand Rapids: Baker Books, 1994.

McGrath, Alister E. *Intellectuals Don't Need God*. Grand Rapids: Zondervan Publishing House, 1993.

Miller, Avigdor. *The Universe Testifies*. Brooklyn: Avigdor Miller, 1995.

Milton, Richard. *The Facts of Life*. London: Corgi Books, 1994.

Morris, Henry M. *The Troubled Waters of Evolution*. San Diego: Creation-Life Publishers, 1977.

Morris, Henry M. *Scientific Creationism*. San Diego: Creation-Life Publishers, 1978.

Morris, Henry M. *Many Infallible Proofs*. El Cajon: Creation Life Publisher, Inc., 1990.

Morris, Henry M. *The Bible and Modern Science*. Chicago: Moody Press, 1968.

Patten, Donald Wesley. *Catastrophism and the Old Testament*. Seattle: Pacific Meridian Publishing Company, 1988.

Pearcey, Nancy R. and Charles B. Thaxton. *The Soul of Science*. Wheaton: Crossway Books, 1994.

Petersen, Dennis R. *Unlocking the Mysteries of Creation*. El Dorado: Creation Resource Publications, 2002.

Phillips, Timothy R. and Dennis L. Okholm. *Christian Apologetics in the Post Modern World*. Downers Grove: InterVarsity Press, 1995.

Rehwinkel, Alfred M. *The Flood*. Saint Louis: Concordia Publishing House, 1951.

Reid, James. *God, The Atom, and the Universe*. Grand Rapids: Zondervan Publishing House, 1971.

Richards, Lawrence O. *It Couldn't Just Happen*. Dallas: Word Publishing, 1989.

Robinson, Gershon and Mordechai Steinman. *The Obvious Proof*. Lakewood: C.I.S. Publishers, 1993.

Ross, Hugh. *The Fingerprint of God*. Orange: Promise Publishing Company, 1991.

Ross, Hugh. *Creation and Time*. Colorado Springs: NavPress Publishing Group, 1994.

Schroeder, Gerald L. *The Hidden Face of God*. New York: Simon and Schuster, 2002.

Schroeder, Gerald L. *The Science of God*. New York: Broadway Books, 1998.

Shedd, William G. T. *Dogmatic Theology*. Nashville: Thomas Nelson Publishers, 1980.

Slifkin, Nosson. *The Science of Torah*. Southfield: Targum Press Inc., 2001.

Spetner, Lee. *Not By Chance*. Brooklyn: The Judaica Press, Inc., 1998.

Stoner, Peter W. and Robert C. Newman. *Science Speaks*. Chicago: Moody Press, 1976.

Stott, John R. W. *You Can Trust the Bible*. Grand Rapids: Discovery House Publishers, 1991.

Taylor, Paul S. *The Illustrated Origins Answer Book*. Gilbert: Eden Communications, 1995.

Varghese, Roy Abraham, ed. *The Intellectuals Speak Out About God*. Chicago: Regnery Gateway, Inc., 1984.

Vos, Howard F., ed. *Can I Trust the Bible?*. Chicago: Moody Press, 1973.

Vos, Howard F. *Can I Really Believe?*. Dallas: Word Publishing, 1995.

Waldman, Shmuel. *Beyond a Reasonable Doubt*. Jerusalem: Feldheim Publishers, 2002.

Whitcomb, John C. *The World That Perished*. Grand Rapids: Baker Book House, 1992.

Whitcomb, John C. and Donald B. DeYoung. *The Moon*. Grand Rapids: Baker Book House, 1978.

Woodson, Leslie. *What You Believe and Why*. Grand Rapids: Zondervan Publishing House, 1972.